MEN, WOMEN & MONEY

NEW ROLES, NEW RULES

GRACE W. WEINSTEIN

NAL BOOKS

NEW AMERICAN LIBRARY

NEW YORK AND SCARBOROUGH, ONTARIO

Published simultaneously in Canada by
The New American Library of Canada Limited

NAL BOOKS TRADEMARK REG. U.S. PAT. OFF. AND FOREIGN COUNTRIES
REGISTERED TRADEMARK—MARCA REGISTRADA
HECHO EN HARRISONBURG, VA., U.S.A.

SIGNET, SIGNET CLASSIC, MENTOR, ONYX, PLUME,
MERIDIAN and NAL BOOKS
are published *in the United States* by New American Library,
1633 Broadway, New York, New York 10019,
in Canada by The New American Library of Canada Limited,
81 Mack Avenue, Scarborough, Ontario M1L 1M8

Library of Congress Cataloging-in-Publication Data

Weinstein, Grace W.
Men, women, and money.

1. Finance, Personal. 2. Women—Finance, Personal.
3. Women—Life skills guides. I. Title.
HG179.W4397   1986   332.024′042   86-12611
ISBN 0-453-00526-8

Designed by Marilyn Ackerman

First Printing, November, 1986

1 2 3 4 5 6 7 8 9

PRINTED IN THE UNITED STATES OF AMERICA

For my family

ACKNOWLEDGMENTS

With warm thanks to everyone who shared both personal stories and professional expertise, including those I interviewed for articles in *Glamour* and *McCall's* and for my earlier books, LIFE PLANS: LOOKING FORWARD TO RETIREMENT and CHILDREN AND MONEY: A PARENTS' GUIDE.

Contents

Introduction

MONEY SHOULD BE simply a tool, used to buy the things we want and need. In truth, it's far more. No matter how much or how little money you may actually have, it's often a substitute for love, an instrument of control, a weapon in interpersonal wars. Little wonder, then, that failure to share basic assumptions about money can damage a relationship beyond repair. Yet people frequently fail to share. It's been said, quite rightly, that money is the last frontier of self-disclosure. We have detailed discussions about the most intimate concerns, but we won't talk about money—what it means to us, how we use and misuse it, where it fits into our lives. If we won't talk about it, even with our nearest and dearest, we shouldn't be surprised when misunderstandings about money intrude on personal relationships.

You have your own money profile and the people in your life have theirs. Since genetics, temperament, and experience are different, you can't expect to respond to money in identical ways. It's not even as simple as one wanting to save and one wanting to spend. You may both want to save—toward different goals and in different ways. You may both want to spend—on different things and at different times. You may laugh at your differences or fight over them, but one way or another they will affect your relationship. This book will help you understand your own money behavior, come to terms with interpersonal differences and make them work for you. It will show you how to use money, and communicate about money, to strengthen your relationships. And it will show you how to deal with personal relationships in a world turned upside down.

New roles for men and women, parents and children, friends and lovers, demand new rules. The "good old days" may or may not have been good, depending on your own perspective, but they certainly were simpler. Men and women used to play the same game by the same rules, back when everyone knew which game they were playing. Young men and women lived in the parental home until they married, and they married fairly young. One breadwinner per family was the norm after marriage, just as two parents per family was only to be expected. Today it's a new ball game. That ball game may be the only one young people know. But it leaves their elders stranded between tradition and innovation, between old roles and new rules.

Today people get married later, if at all, and may have one or more live-together relationships first. Two incomes are relied upon, even after children are born, as aspirations outpace income. Divorce and remarriage lead to extended families and multiple obligations, both financial and emotional. Older adults try to prepare for their own retirement while caring for their own aging parents.

We are currently in a stage of transition. In another decade, it's possible that we'll have it all sorted out. Perhaps we'll know how to combine two careers with parenting and make it work. Maybe we'll work out property distributions in divorce so that they are fair to everyone. We may even, in this golden age to come, be able to deal with our parents and our children and our partners without letting money be divisive.

Meanwhile, in this world turned upside down by social and economic change, we need rules to live by. We need, at the very least, a heavy dose of common sense to help us manage the financial affairs within our intimate relationships. Hence this book. Whether you are in your twenties or your sixties, single or married, divorced or widowed or remarried, this book will help you find your way amidst the monetary mine fields. It will help you work out the complexities of property ownership and management in different kinds of relationships while providing the negotiating techniques you need to make life run smoothly.

If you've ever puzzled over the role of money in a relationship—how to divvy expenses with a roommate, work out a two-income budget as a married couple, combine career and child-rearing as young parents or be both parent to your children and child to your parents—this book is for you.

· 1 ·

Men, Women, and Money

IN AUGUST 1984 husband-wife finances were front page news. Vice-presidential candidate Geraldine Ferraro, reporters discovered, had neglected to separate her financial affairs from those of her husband John Zaccaro. The subject, for a while, was a joke; who, the electorate wanted to know, actually owned the family refrigerator?

Does *any* couple know who "owns" the family refrigerator? Does *any* couple so separate their finances that neither takes responsibility for, or even knows anything about, the other's pocketbook?

Ferraro and Zaccaro were, after all, married. What's more, they had married in 1960, at a time when husbands and wives always—or almost always—commingled their finances. What was different, now, was that Ferraro was suddenly thrust into the national political spotlight. The press always scrutinized a candidate's finances, but in this case the issue was different because the candidate was a woman. The *wives* of past candidates had seldom had independent financial affairs to subject to the public spotlight. The *husbands* of candidates are another story.

Public interest in Ferraro-Zaccaro finances, and those finances themselves, may now seem like a footnote to history. But that footnote says a great deal about male-female relationships in the 1980s, about how those relationships are affected by money, and how money, in turn, affects those relationships.

Money *is* important. It's important because it's a medium

1

of exchange, the useful tool we use to buy the things we need and want. But it's also important because, beyond being a useful tool, it's a symbol of a great many other things. It's as a symbol, for the most part, that money plays such a significant role in the relationships between men and women.

You are probably not a political candidate. You can probably feel secure in the fact that no one outside your immediate family (with the exception, of course, of the IRS) cares a fig about your personal finances. But what about *within* your family? How many times have money or attitudes toward money or behaviors with money affected your most personal relationships?

We all have hang-ups over money. We think about money a great deal, worry about it, argue about it. Many of us, according to a 1985 *Money* magazine survey, are more preoccupied with money than with sex—although we do (thank goodness!) enjoy sex more. We spend and save, sometimes inconsistently, in ways that give us pleasure, build our self-esteem, heighten our sense of security. But those ways may not always be the ways of our nearest and dearest. And that's when sparks can fly. Witness . . .

. . . She throws a surprise party for his birthday; he complains of the cost;

. . . He uses eight different credit cards, juggling bills at the end of every month; she prefers to pay cash;

. . . She thinks her income is hers to spend while his supports the family; he believes both incomes should be shared and shared alike;

. . . He takes a fling in commodity futures; she shudders and sticks to certificates of deposit;

. . . She wants to pay her own way on dates; he refuses. Or she, unsure of his reaction, doesn't offer to share the costs and he stops calling;

. . . He lets bills pile up and is careless about recording checks; she prefers to pay bills as they come in and is a meticulous record-keeper;

. . . She wants help from parents to buy a house now; he is adamant about waiting and going it alone;

. . . His greatest pleasure is watching his bank balance grow; she prefers to spend money on life's pleasures;

. . . She moves in with him, expecting to share expenses, and he hands her the rent bill;

. . . He sends his own child to Europe for the summer but suggests that his stepdaughter will enjoy day camp at the Y.

The examples are endless. Whether there is too little money, or too much, people argue over its disposition. Buying a new camera is often not a question of what kind of camera to buy and how much it costs; instead, in many relationships, it becomes an issue of who makes the decision and who exerts control. Buying that camera, unless both partners agree, ignites the tinder of differing values. "You always buy what you want" or "Why a camera when we need a new rug?" or "How will we *ever* have enough money to buy a house?"

When people argue over money, in short, the argument is likely to have little to do with money. The actors may change—male and female, young and old, single or married or single again—but the underlying scenario is the same. That scenario almost always has to do with issues of control, security, self-esteem, and, above all, love. We don't talk about money in these terms. We may not talk about money, as such, at all. But our arguments about money and our behavior with money frequently reflect our underlying feelings about ourselves and about the world. An understanding that this is so can help in handling both personal finances and personal relationships. Understanding the symbolism is an essential start.

Money symbolizes control. It is the medium of exchange in a struggle for power. Spoken or unspoken, it's often a matter of "I'm making the money (or, these days, I'm making *more* money) so I'm in charge here." Or, as

Psychology Today magazine phrased it in summing up a 1981 survey on money, "Men and women have used money to attract and control each other ever since it was invented."

Money symbolizes security. Having enough money, of course, is real security. But *feeling* that you have enough money, that you are secure, is a different matter. Sometimes it's a matter of being cared for, sometimes it's a question of who's earning what. But the same dollar income can produce feelings of security or of insecurity, and it's not a matter of life-style so much as of psychological comfort.

Money symbolizes self-esteem in a society that values people according to their earning power, and self-esteem plays an important role in human relationships. People who don't think well of themselves—because they don't earn as much as they'd like to or as much as their spouses or as much as they once did—frequently have problems sustaining fulfilling relationships.

Money symbolizes love. Special care lavished on a gift is a loving gesture. But some people can show love only by giving money and material things; others feel that they are loved only when they receive such tangible tokens. The child who receives "things" as the primary evidence of parental love may grow up to be the adult who needs to be reassured of love through frequent gifts. What happens when that adult pairs off with someone who fails to see the connection between love and material things?

Individual Differences

Although the money-talk scenario is much the same for people of both sexes and all ages and marital status, there are also significant differences related to individual temperament, to gender, and to generation.

Temperament is a volatile factor in the money equation. Although much money behavior is learned, innate temperament—the qualities we're born with—shapes that learning. You can see personality differences in children. Infants range across a spectrum from passive to aggressive, reacting to stimuli in sharply different ways. Among school-age children, those who toss money around, are free spenders and generous to a fault, are also often outgoing souls, open to friendship and to new experiences. Others are conservative, reluctant to let go of money at all and cautious about new experiences. The patterns often continue into adulthood, with predictable results when one marries the other. Differences in temperament may be one reason why husbands and wives see things differently. Ask a husband and wife who makes most decisions, for instance, and you might think they are reporting on two different marriages. As sociologist Jessie Bernard put it in her classic work, *The Future of Marriage*, every marriage is actually two marriages, his and hers; they intersect but they are not the same. Spouses perceive circumstances differently, as Dr. Bernard points out, through the prism of each one's needs, values, attitudes, and beliefs.

But innate temperament can be modified, if not entirely changed. Parents shape their children's behavior with money. And spouses often influence each other. A free-spending husband may spend a bit less freely as the years go by, tempered by his wife's cautious nature; she, in turn, may begin to spend a bit more freely till they're more and more alike. Some partnerships, of course, dissolve over intrinsically opposed attitudes toward money. And other partners remain at opposite poles, but learn to coexist in a loving relationship.

Gender is one of the most important factors, simply because of the ways in which men and women are (still) brought up to fulfill distinct and specific roles. In some families girls receive allowances because they are expected to be independent and to earn their own money. In other families, boys receive allowances because they need money to spend on a regular basis, while girls do not because, if they must ask for it as needed, parents can retain control. The result: Girls learn to be dependent. They also, too often, learn to be manipulative in coaxing money from parents. And they lose (or never gain) the self-esteem that comes with being independent.

Little has changed in American child-rearing practices, despite a decade and more of the women's movement. A study conducted in late 1984 by researchers at the University of Minnesota and Ohio State University found that a third of the teenage girls studied and about half of the teenage boys had high self-esteem; the figures are almost exactly the same as a comparable study conducted fifteen years earlier. Despite fifteen years of lip service to equality, in other words, girls still give way to others in an effort to be popular and boys still assert their independence.

This pattern—and this lack of self-esteem—often carry over into adult relationships. Even today, when a sharp increase in the number of working wives has dramatically raised the living standards of millions of families, the pattern continues. It's evident in the husband who gives his wife a strictly allocated household allowance, in the wife who consults her husband about any more-than-minor expenditure, in the woman who is content with a low-level job or with no job at all because, she insists, she "has no skills anyone would want."

This familiar pattern of male dominance and female submissiveness works well for many couples. Marriage is such a delicate web of dependence and interdependence that partners make all sorts of adjustments and compromises in order to make the marriage work. Sometimes those adjustments take the form of an otherwise successful woman deferring to her husband; sometimes it's a matter of an otherwise assertive man consulting his wife. Whatever works in a particular relationship is whatever works—unless and until the winds of change affect one partner more than the other. There may not be an accurate count of how many marriages broke up in the wake of the women's movement, but it seems clear, at least to this observer, that many marriages simply couldn't survive changing attitudes toward male-female roles, changes that are frequently enacted on the financial front. When a woman who never paid attention to financial matters begins to ask questions, when she wants to know what's on the tax return before she signs it, her husband may feel threatened. When she begins to assert herself about money, when she decides, for example, that joint ownership isn't always a good idea, the marriage itself may be threatened.

Generation is relevant here as well. The economic climate and the changing social scene affect the different generations in different ways.

One of the biggest elements in today's social scene is the increasing number of women in the work force. In 1960 approximately 30 percent of married women held jobs outside the home; by 1984 the official figure was 53 percent. But, as pointed out by the Conference Board, a business research group, the real figure in families where the husband has not yet retired is closer to 65 percent. These working wives are pushing their families into upper income brackets while they themselves become much more confident with money. But newfound confidence isn't limited to married women. Single women, frequently marrying much later than their mothers did, are in the labor force in far greater numbers than ever before. For women under age 25, a *Glamour* magazine survey reported in January 1985, "One of the most marked trends in the past three years is the ever-increasing importance of financial success as a personal goal." That goal, whether or not the respondents are currently married, is bound to affect their relationships with the men in their lives.

The way you regard money has a lot to do with whether you earn it for yourself. It also has a lot to do with how much money your parents had, their attitudes toward that money, and the era in which you grew up. Attitudes are key. If your parents moaned about poverty when they actually had money to spend, you may spend your life looking over your shoulder for a wolf that isn't there. If your father doled out money to your mother, and she consulted with him on every major purchase, you may give lip service to equality but feel most comfortable repeating the pattern.

But the economic climate in which you came to maturity is also significant. Look at any three-generation family, including your own. You're very likely to find grandparents shaped by the Depression, fearful of debt and concerned with safety. These are the people who didn't invest because they had little money to invest; today they want their savings insured. These are also couples with an established pattern of male breadwinner–female homemaker, a pattern that may suit both partners. Women in this age group may make a lot of the day-to-day financial decisions, but they frequently defer to their husbands in such "masculine" areas as investments, insurance, and major purchases. Men, in turn, expect to make these decisions without challenge and without consultation. Women over 60, not suprisingly, were found by a recent Investment Company Institute survey to have the lowest levels of joint responsibility and to be more likely to leave financial planning to their husbands. Women in this generation, also not at all surprisingly, are very likely to be impoverished by widowhood or divorce.

The middle generation came to maturity and thrived in the economic boom of the 1950s and 1960s; they believe, as an article of faith, that life will always get better and better. Members of this generation spend money in the here-and-now but, well tutored by their parents, balance that spending with an eye to the future. They look ahead to retirement, by and large, with cautious optimism.

But it's this middle generation, couples now in their forties and fifties, who have felt the brunt of social change. Women who once accepted the occupational role of wife-and-mother suddenly found that the rules had changed, that the role was no longer universally respected. Since the change often came at a time when the children were in school all day or when the nest was entirely empty, many of these women, their consciousnesses raised, returned to the work force. Their husbands, however, had not had their consciousness raised. Many objected. Or, if they didn't object, they didn't know quite what to make of the new women their wives had become. Earning an independent income makes a person independent. "It's *my* life, *my* time, *my* money" is the way one woman described her new sense of self. Newfound independence on the part of one partner, without corresponding change on the part of the other, upsets the equilibrium of a marriage. Some wives left the family fold, newly intent on "finding themselves," leaving confused and distraught husbands behind. Some husbands left instead, angry at unexpected and undesired changes in the women they thought they knew.

The third generation is another story altogether. Totally tuned in to the present, using credit to vastly expand their purchasing power, today's young adults seem to see little point in saving. Whether they see the point or not, they may find it difficult to save—or they may find their saving forced into specific channels. As economist Arnold Kling pointed out in *The Wall Street Journal* in early 1986, Social Security taxes alone consume considerable income. Where a couple jointly earning $60,000 a year in 1960 paid $1,000 in Social Security taxes, he notes, a couple with the same joint income in 1985 paid $4,200 toward Social Security. The $3,200 difference, over 5 percent of gross income, might otherwise be saved or invested. Housing is another culprit, and we don't have to go back as far back as 1960 to see drastic change. Urban Institute analysts Frank Levy and Richard C. Michel point out that in 1973 the typical 30-year-old put 21 percent of take-home pay toward housing; today that typical 30-year-old is putting 44 percent toward housing. The older generation, those who already own their homes, benefited from recent housing price appreciation; all it's meant to the younger generation is higher housing costs.

This young generation clearly suffers from what has been called downward mobility—although it may be more a case of lowered expectations. Although the 76-

million-plus men and women in the "baby boom" generation have more apparent spending power than their
parents did at the same age, their earnings often don't
match their expectations. Costs have outpaced earnings
growth over the last decade. Salaries have begun to stag-
nate, forced down in part by the tremendous surge of
baby boomers into the job market, where they compete
with each other, and in part by a worldwide economic
slowdown.

Americans always expect to earn more and live better
than their parents. They certainly expect to live at least
as well. Yet the baby boom generation, through no fault
of its own, is falling behind. Unable to afford a house,
postponing parenthood, dependent on two incomes,
people in their twenties and thirties often feel economically deprived. They may not actually be deprived in
absolute terms—rising expectations can fuel frustration,
as yesterday's luxuries become today's necessities—but
that feeling can provoke feelings of inadequacy and result
in conflict.

This is also the generation most marked by shifts in
male-female relationships, more likely to regard marriage as an equal partnership. Only 37 percent of the
women and 43 percent of the men responding to a 1985
Roper Poll for Philip Morris want a traditional marriage
in which the husband is the sole provider and the wife
runs the house; in 1974 more than half of the respondents, men and women alike, opted for the traditional. In
many of today's young couples, where both husbands
and wives fully expect wives to work outside the home,
both are independent. It's entirely possible that no one
is cooking and cleaning—pick-up meals and sporadic
attacks at dust may be the rule—but both partners earn
income and both share in decisions about spending that
income. When one spouse is chiefly responsible for financial decisions, according to the Investment Company
Institute study, that spouse is frequently the wife. "There
was a time not long ago when working women still left
the 'big' money decisions up to their husbands," says

author Caroline Bird, commenting on the 1985 *Glamour* survey. "I think that pattern will never even occur to women who are now in their twenties." There may still be different attitudes toward money and what money does, with resulting conflict, but power and control are less likely to be the issues.

Individuals differ, of course, as do relationships. Some elderly women are more financially astute and independent than their granddaughters. Some partners share values and assumptions, so that conflict over money is rare. People move in and out of different relationships in different life stages; at various times in your life you may be single, married, divorced, widowed, remarried. These life stages have both financial and emotional ramifications. But by and large, economic considerations coupled with rapid social change have subjected today's male-female relationships, inside and outside of marriage, to increasing levels of tension. Money is often the vehicle through which that tension is expressed.

· 2 ·

The Single State

YOU MAY be single by choice, uninterested in marriage, or delaying it for the time being. You may be single by chance, because you haven't yet married (although you would like to), or because a marriage ended in separation or divorce. Either way, you have a lot of company. Almost a quarter of all American households are now one-person households, a proportion that has tripled in forty years, almost doubled in the last fifteen.

Why so many one-person households? There are many reasons. Among them: Young people are marrying later, not till a median age, in 1985, of 25.5 for men and 23.3 for women. That's the highest age at first marriage for men since 1900, when it was 25.9, and the highest age for women ever recorded. These young adults don't want to remain in their parents' homes in the years between schooling and marriage (although this trend has reversed slightly since 1980 as more young adults, perhaps for economic reasons, do remain with their parents). And they are earning enough, a great many of them, to live independently. Adults of all ages are leaving unhappy marriages and, although most remarry, are living alone in the interim. And older folk, especially women, are frequently left alone by the death of a partner.

Money plays different roles in these singles' lives. Young singles, even though relatively few are the affluent "Yuppies" of the popular press (a minuscule 5 percent, according to *American Demographics* magazine), do have sizable amounts of discretionary income. They may be squeezing

12

every penny to afford rent on their own apartments, but, without dependents to support, they can spend the rest of their incomes on pleasure. What's more, they'll use credit to do so and worry about payment later. "Sure, I go skiing two or three times a winter," says an advertising copywriter. "Why should I put the money in the bank?"

Young adults feel flush with newfound financial independence and, in truth, most can expect at least a decade of steadily rising income as they become increasingly competent on the job and move into positions of responsibility. A solid income base in these years should make it possible to save, invest, and plan for the future. Instead, many young singles not only live up to the hilt of each paycheck but mortgage their future with ever-higher levels of debt. If this kind of self-indulgent singlehood continues for any period of time, money patterns may well be established that could carry over into later life and create conflict. Whether one marries or not, self-indulgence in the early years can lead to financial insecurity in the later years—and to relationships that founder on the shoals of insecurity.

What may be a problem, too, is that you may not be doing as well as you think you are. This generation of young adults, says *The Wall Street Journal*, "is caught in a squeeze between spiraling costs and stagnating salaries." People now in their thirties caught the gold ring before the carousel slowed, securing a competitive edge in the job market before the baby boom bulge moved in. Those a few years younger aren't so lucky. Inflation masked the setbacks of the last decade, but there has, in fact, been a real decline in income. Many people in this age group, as a result, will never catch up. They'll never be able to attain the living standards of their parents, according to Robert Hopkins, an economist with Chase Econometrics, or even of their counterparts of ten years earlier. In an effort to catch up, careers are being firmly established before marriage, parenthood is being postponed, and two-income couples are the norm.

Money Stages for Singles

The way money is handled is not necessarily the same, of course, among singles in their twenties and those who remain single into their thirties and forties. It's very different for those who become single in their sixties or seventies.

The younger set may be sharing cramped living quarters with several friends, or still living with parents because income and rent are incompatible. Yet this group is also the target, often a willing target, for purveyors of health food, fitness clubs and spas, and electronic gadgets—all the "good things" of life. Half the single women in one survey by *Ms.* magazine said it was "very easy" to spend money for entertainment; only 38 percent of the married respondents felt the same.

At the same time many singles have trouble spending money on themselves, perhaps because life seems incomplete and temporary before marriage. Single men often get themselves into financial trouble, says Des Moines financial planner Sylvia DeWitt, because they want to impress women by paying for everything when they go out. They don't make enough, even without spending much on themselves, to support this life-style. Single women may wait for marriage, marking time instead of making financial plans. When these singles wake up, sometimes well into their forties, half a life span has gone by.

Older singles, those in their thirties and forties, are still a marketing target and still spend money on personal goods and services, but they also tend to become more settled. "I'm not a 'single,' " as one woman puts it; "that implies someone irresponsible, a swinger. Let's just say I'm an unmarried grown-up." As a grown-up, she has bought her own co-op apartment and is starting an investment program. If you're single, as a mature adult, you too should build a solid financial foundation.

Today more and more single women refuse to remain in a holding pattern, waiting for "Mr. Right" to come

along. More and more single men want to go beyond
what one calls a "dorm style" of living. Instead, both
men and women are doing whatever it takes to make life
comfortable in the here-and-now. "No more hand-me-
downs," as one New Yorker puts it. "I don't have to be
married to enjoy setting a good table and sitting on comfortable furniture." Capitalizing on this trend, advertisers are targeting this market. *Self* magazine recently started
a gift registry for singles. Single men and women, reports
the trade journal *Adweek*, "are buying items that used
to be reserved for the married." Single men and women
can also, if they're smart, set investment goals for the
future.

The picture with once-again singles is a bit different.
Whether you've been divorced or widowed, after all,
you're likely to have the material things you want. What
you may not have had before, however, is financial freedom. Money may be tight, in the aftermath of divorce
or death, but you can manage it well or poorly, by yourself and for yourself, without accounting to anyone else.
That may be a mixed blessing, if you are impoverished
by circumstance or if you would simply prefer to be
married, but forced singlehood also forces some money
know-how. "I never paid any attention to money while
I was married. My husband handled everything," one
divorcée notes. "Now I'm taking a course on managing
money because I want to do it right. I have to take the
responsibility. My money, such as it is, is mine."

The oldest group of singles, largely women, is created
by death. These women are self-sufficient, for the most
part, with over 80 percent maintaining their own households. But many are poor, or close to it, subsisting on
Social Security, perhaps a pension, occasional help from
children. Planning ahead for these later years is addressed
in Chapter 9.

Whether single by choice or by chance, whether initially or once again, whether living alone or with others,
young and middle-aged singles face particular love-and-
money complications. Living together as a prelude to or

substitute for marriage, as contrasted to sharing quarters for economic reasons, has become such an important phenomenon of the 1980s that it will be the focus of Chapter 3. This chapter goes into money hang-ups involving parents, friends, roommates, and social companions (for want of a better term; "date" seems so archaic).

Parental Ties

The young adult, once out of school and earning an income, isn't necessarily free of the ties that bind. Emotionally and financially, parent-child links continue. Asserting financial independence is an essential part of growing up, but that doesn't mean that it is easy to do. The relationship between young adults and their parents, in fact, often resembles a seesaw. The child, at one end, alternates between security and independence; the parents, on the other, shift between holding on and letting go.

It's particularly difficult when you continue to live in your parents' home. In 1984, according to the Census Bureau, 54 percent of 18- to 24-year-olds were still living at home, compared to 47.3 percent of this age group in 1970. Among 25- to 34-year-olds, 10.4 percent were still at home in 1984, against 8 percent in 1970. The high cost of housing is one reason, along with expectations for a standard of living that can't be met on a starting salary. Parents seem almost resigned (although, if you read Chapter 8, you'll understand their perspective on the matter). While 40 percent of the older generation moved away from home before age 21, according to the 1985 *Money* magazine survey, only 20 percent think their children will be out by the same age.

If you remain at home, for whatever reason, you should try to renegotiate your relationship with your parents so that you can interact as adults. If you return home after living on your own, you should do the same. Curfews should be out, but mutual consideration—including information about whether or not you'll be home for

meals—should definitely be in. You'll find it easier to
come to terms with your parents, and to interact as adults,
if you share both the work and the costs of running the
household. It isn't fair to expect free room and board,
just because you've always had it; you've "always" been
a child. You can become a grown-up by doing as Jill, a
fledgling copywriter does: "I pay rent and my own phone
bill, as well as my personal expenses; I also cook dinner
at least once a week and get together with my mother
once a month for general housecleaning." Sit down with
your parents and discuss what they expect and what you
are able and willing to do; then live up to the agreement.

Moving out, establishing your own household, doesn't
necessarily eliminate the independence seesaw. You may
feel more than ready to move out, eager for the independence implicit in a place of your own. Your parents
may be eager to have you do so, recognizing your need
to be independent. Yet you may feel insecure as you
spread your wings for the first time, inclined to lean on
your parents at least occasionally for support. They, in
turn, may long for the privacy that the empty nest represents but still be unsure that you can really make it
on your own. The conflicts show up in ways big and
small. As Anne proudly shows off her first apartment,
she says, "I did every bit of it myself. My mother wanted
to buy me a couch, but I wouldn't let her." Her mother
notes, "I was delighted when Anne wanted to get her
own apartment and furnish it herself. But how can I let
her live with hand-me-downs and make-dos when I can
make things so much easier for her and never notice the
cost?"

Moving out, of course, doesn't mean the apron strings
are broken. They may be stretched. And they may snap
back into place. It all depends on both your parents'
attitude and your own. It's particularly difficult when
your parents insist on giving. "It's very seductive," says
Tilla Vahanian, Ed.D., a psychotherapist in private practice in New York, "but if you really want to be independent you have to take responsibility for not being

seduced." That may be easier said than done. One young woman, whose father insists on providing her with a large, heavy automobile so she'll be "safe," does not want to hurt his feelings by rejecting the gift. But she should examine those feelings. Is she accepting the car because she enjoys being Daddy's little girl, and having him worry about her? Or is she accepting the car temporarily, know-ing—and telling him—that it isn't the one she wants, until she can afford her own choice? And, for that matter, is her father giving her the car truly in the interests of safety? Or does he want to retain control? Money *is* control and gifts can be a way of saying "As long as I pay the bills, you'll do what I think is right."

Whatever your parents may want, you can't just blame them for keeping you a child. They can't do it alone. You have to cooperate, consciously or unconsciously. Thus, if you accept gifts or money from your parents after you are presumably on your own, you should ask yourself, "Am I accepting this out of a wish to cling, a fear of independence? Or am I taking it as a freely given gift between equals?" If you respect your parents and your-self, says Dr. Vahanian, then you can tell them, "This gift is not appropriate and I can't accept it—but that doesn't mean I don't love you." Or with mutual respect you can also say, "Thank you. I will accept this gift and continue to do as I think best for me."

A lot depends, of course, on whether you can really manage to be financially independent. If you can't, ide-ally, you should be able to accept proffered help without falling into emotional dependence. This is often easier after independence is well established. If you need finan-cial help to move out of your parents' home in the first place, the ground rules of mutual autonomy will be harder to set. Your parents may continue to think of you as a child, and you may continue to feel like a child.

In today's economy, of course, it's entirely possible to shift from independence to dependence and back again. You may decide your first career field isn't right after all; you may lose a job in a company consolidation; you may decide further schooling is essential. If you do need financial assistance to make it through a tough stretch and your parents have offered help with no strings attached, it makes sense to accept; real independence should not be confused with a foolhardy act of rebellion. In fact, if you rebel like an adolescent, refusing help while you're trying to establish yourself on your own, you may end up slinking back to the parental fold, as dependent as ever. For some, notes Howard Halpern, Ph.D., a psychologist and author of *No Strings Attached*, this may even be the unconscious intent, as in: "I couldn't swing it, so I'll be a little girl again."

There's a great deal of comfort, of course, in knowing that your parents are ready to back you up financially and emotionally in the event of an emergency. The question is, what is an emergency? Rent money when you are out of work is one thing; rent money so you can afford a nicer place is another. Paying for car insurance is helpful, but not necessarily essential; paying for medical care may stand between you and Medicaid. You have to decide, for your own sake, exactly where to draw the line. "To know that you have a supportive, available connection is terribly important," Dr. Vahanian points out. "But taking subsidy for granted is destructive because it removes the motivation to be self-reliant."

What is *your* situation? Are you really enjoying the security of remaining dependent? Are your parents, consciously or unconsciously, trying to keep you dependent and therefore close? Remember, it always takes two to tango. You should examine your own motivation and that of your parents in general terms. And you should look at specific gifts in terms of whether there are strings attached. Does giving you a car mean that you must be available to take your mother on errands? Or that you will run over and visit on a regular basis? Does subsidizing your rent mean that you are expected to make dinner for your parents every Sunday?

There may be a hidden message, and it may not be obvious. But don't leap to conclusions. Your parents may delight in seeing you on a regular basis, but that may not be why they are giving you a car or subsidizing your rent. In order to be sure, however, you should always get any conditions of an offer out on the table. If the offer involves cash, ask some hard questions: Is this a loan or a gift? If it's a loan, when is it to be repaid? Is there any interest? If you don't get the answers to these questions, right at the outset, there may be hard feelings later on. "My parents provided the cash for the down payment on my condo," says an insurance underwriter. "I thought it was a gift, but it turned out five years later that they were very angry with me because I'd received a promotion and hadn't offered to pay them back. I had considered making the offer, but I honestly thought they'd be insulted if I did."

Get both your parents' expectations (*both* your parents, since they may disagree) and your own out in the open and don't be surprised if some ambivalence surfaces. Your parents may sincerely want to see you out of the nest and be willing to make unconditional gifts toward that end. At the same time, on some level they may want to keep the relationship you've had; that means keeping you dependent and means a gift intended to control. Money, and the gifts it buys, is never a simple commodity. It can be a stand-in for love, and the withholding of money can mean the withholding of love. With or without love, money is an obvious instrument for control, easily becoming the focus of what Dr. Halpern calls the "money minuet," those intergenerational songs and dances about financial dependence.

As one mother put it in *No Strings Attached*, in extending an invitation to the money minuet: "I don't want you living in that neighborhood. Why don't we buy a co-op apartment for you in a safe building in a safe neighborhood? We'll own it, but for all intents and purposes it will be yours. Maybe Dad and I will stay over occasionally if we come into the city for the theater or something." It isn't hard to hear the real message here. Accept the offer, generous as it is, and you're likely to have Mom and Dad feeling free to visit, with or without warning, as it suits them.

If your parents give in to the temptation and set conditions when they offer a gift, remember that once you are on your own they have every right to feel they owe you nothing. If they do help, it's because they choose to do so, and they are therefore free to impose restrictions. "They have a perfect right to say 'I'll only do it if you'll wear purple dresses from now on,' " says Dr. Halpern. "They have a perfect right to say whatever they want. It may be crazy, it may be inconsiderate, it may be too restrictive, but they have a right to say it." You, in turn, have the right to refuse both the restrictions and the offer. It's a package deal.

Although it may not seem so now, if you are in your early twenties and making the first move away from your parents' home, the seesaw will stabilize with time. As you become more and more independent, both financially and emotionally, you will probably move on to an adult-to-adult relationship with your parents. As one woman in her late twenties puts it: "When I was younger I had to prove I didn't need anything they gave me. Now I don't need it, so it's okay to want and to take occasionally." What should happen, in the end, is that you and your parents establish the right distance. You and they should, in an ideal world, remain loving and close while at the same time being independent adults.

The world, of course, isn't always ideal. Many adults in their forties and fifties still dance the money minuet with their parents. Some of those issues will be addressed in later chapters. For young singles, meanwhile, trying to establish financial and emotional independence, it may help to remember that it seldom happens quickly. The whole process of entering adulthood lasts from about age seventeen to age thirty-three, according to Daniel Levinson, Ph.D., a pioneer in the study of adult development and the author of *The Seasons of a Man's Life.* The process—becoming financially and emotionally less dependent on your parents, loosening the apron strings so that you can become a self-reliant adult—is the focus of your life during this period. You needn't, and you probably can't, cut those strings all at once. But you should bear in mind that the pattern of your adult life is, at least to some extent, now being set. If you continue to be dependent long after you are out of school and working, you are developing a habit that may be difficult to break and a dependence that goes beyond money to parental approval. "You cannot feel really independent," Dr. Vahanian points out, "unless you are comfortable with the decisions you make. Money is just one dimension." It's a sign of independence, in short, to be able to make your own choices. *You* must decide where you want to live and what kind of car you want to drive, without regard to whether or not your parents approve.

Friendship

Researchers at the Institute of Social Research, University of Michigan, recently studied the question: "Do today's 'independent lifestyles' reflect a trend toward social isolation and a consequent threat to health and well-being?" The underlying assumption was that living alone and the resulting social isolation led to generally lower levels of well-being among the unmarried. But the results were a surprise to the researchers, although probably not to you. With the exception of single mothers, whose lives left little opportunity for social contacts, other singles were doing just fine. In fact, as reported in the ISR Newsletter, "Rather than experiencing social isolation, many people who lived alone showed signs of a 'compensation' phenomenon: They had many more contacts outside the household than did people who lived with others." Living alone is frequently a matter of choice, the researchers concluded, but people who live alone by choice also usually choose to have a wide network of social contacts outside the home.

Unless you're a confirmed hermit, in other words, you need some social interaction. When you don't have that interaction on the home front, you seek it elsewhere. Friends are important to everyone, but when you live alone, friends are likely to play a vital part in your life. And those friends are people with whom you may have financial interactions as well.

By "financial interactions," I don't simply mean borrowing or lending money. Friends *do* occasionally borrow from each other, with mixed results which we'll discuss in a bit. But financial implications also surface in other areas: matching lifestyles, financial compatibility, and roommate relationships.

Matching life-styles may become a problem only when economic incompatibility takes place. Friendships often start out on an equal level; you become friends with people you meet at school or at work or through other friends, so that, at least at the outset, income levels and interests may be much the same. Jane and Laura strike up a friendship during their management training program; as trainees their income is the same and, as recent college graduates, their interests are about the same. "We shop for clothes together because we both need more 'dress-for-success' suits," Jane says, "and our budgets are about the same. We both instinctively turn away from things that cost too much, and we define 'too much' the same way."

But what happens five years down the road? If Laura has had three promotions, with sizable raises, while Jane plods steadily ahead, does the friendship survive? It might, if they're in different offices so that Laura isn't now in a supervisory position over Jane. But the relationship may deteriorate anyway if Laura always chooses expensive restaurants when they go out to lunch, leaving Jane uncomfortable about picking up her share of the check, or if Laura rattles on about her latest trip to Guadeloupe while Jane spends her vacations at the Jersey Shore, or if Laura sports a new VCR while Jane watches television on a set handed down from her parents' home. It's not just that Laura moved ahead on the job; friendship seldom ends for just that reason. Nor is it simply that Laura is being insensitive in flaunting her new affluence. She is being insensitive, of course, but the problem lies deeper. Status is so important to Laura, status measured through conspicuous consumption, that she can't restrain her spending or her talk of spending even in the company of Jane, whose friendship she values. So as Laura lives up to every penny of her new income, the foundation for friendship is threatened. Friends have to be able to do things with each other, share experiences, visit comfortably in each other's homes. Sometimes all this is possible across income and affluence lines, if mutual interests and mutual supportiveness are strong enough. But, for many people, it simply doesn't work. "Even if Laura agrees to meet in the deli for lunch," Jane notes, "I just don't feel comfortable with her any more. We've grown too far apart."

As with any money relationships, attitude may count even more than income. Friends may not even *know* each other's incomes, once out of the starting gate with careers well launched. New college grads, flush with excitement during the recruiting and hiring process, may share information about starting salaries, but most adults won't reveal what they earn to anyone but a spouse (and some won't even do that). They don't tell their parents, and they don't tell their friends. Men are more reticent than women, probably because women don't earn nearly as much. In a 1981 *Psychology Today* survey, 44 percent of male respondents and 53 percent of female had shared information about income with friends. When the income was over $50,000, however, the overall percentage willing to squeal dropped to 28 percent.

Money has often been said to be the last taboo. Ask about my sex life, ask me if I beat my dog, but don't ask how much I earn. Institutionalized procedures buttress our own sense of secrecy; many corporations, for example, insist that employees keep their salaries to themselves.

So Laura and Jane may not even know each other's income. They can still judge relative affluence. And their friendship might have deteriorated rapidly or never even begun if, instead of income incompatibility, they had suffered from attitude incompatibility. Assume, for a moment, that their career paths and their incomes remained virtually identical but that Laura pinched her pennies while Jane enjoyed the good things in life. Jane might laugh affectionately at Laura's penny-pinching— until too many ducked luncheon checks take their toll. It's hard to concentrate on a friend's sterling qualities when miserliness gets in the way. Or, as put by David Michaelis, author of *The Best of Friends,* "It's a matter of priorities. We will resent the friend who is cheap with his money when we think he doesn't need to be. Conversely, we'll be annoyed by the friend who insists on spending extravagantly when we clearly can't afford to go along."

Neither a Borrower...

An income gap between friends can become a chasm when one borrows money from the other . . . not the $5 or $10 here or there when cash flow is tight, but the larger loan that points up a real disparity. The problem is not the money, not if the lender can spare the cash, but a subtle shift in the balance of the relationship. The borrower, no matter how genuine or how temporary the need, loses self-esteem in the process of asking. The lender, no matter how sincere the willingness to give, feels uncomfortable at money being injected into the relationship. Finances have no place in friendship, we're taught from an early age, and their intrusion can harm the friendship. "Rosalie was the only person I could turn to when I had heavy uninsured medical expenses. We'd been close for so many years that I thought she'd understand," one woman comments. "She lent me the money I needed, I paid her back as soon as I could, but our friendship has never been the same since."

There's often a degree of discomfort, on the part of both borrower and lender, stemming from their own inner feelings about money. Yet rejecting a friend's request for money isn't the answer either. It's a question of "damned if you do, damned if you don't," because once money rears its head, friendship is likely to cool.

Sometimes, of course, the friendship ceases to exist for reasons that may or may not be related to the loan. I've received quite a few letters from readers of my *Good Housekeeping* column wanting to know how—and if—they can recover a debt from a former friend who has either disappeared or become unresponsive. A typical letter reads: "My friend borrowed $1,000 to buy a truck and promised to pay me back within six months. But he moved away, he won't answer my letters, and I don't know what to do." There's not a lot she can do, after the fact, although a written record of the loan or witnesses to a verbal agreement may help collection via small claims court. It's not pleasant, but when the loan involves more than you can afford to lose and a friend has proven to be the fair weather variety, this may be the only course to take.

Real friendship can usually be salvaged, despite financial need, if you can divorce money from its emotional content. Look at the loan as a business arrangement, and treat it in a businesslike way. If a friend requests a start-up loan for a business or help with a down payment—anything where real money is involved—put the agreement in writing, with copies for each of you. Include all the agreed-upon terms: how much is borrowed, how much interest is due (if any; think carefully about charging interest to a friend), and the anticipated repayment date. Then you'll both be able to treat the matter objectively, giving you a better chance of holding onto a valued friendship. And you'll be sure of repayment even if the borrower should die before the debt is paid.

Roommate Relationships

If living alone gets to be too much for you, either financially or emotionally, you may want to consider tak-

ing a roommate. Sharing living quarters, however, even
when there is no romantic entanglement, poses pitfalls
of its own.

Assume that you've worked out your own budget, and
you know how much you can afford to spend on rent.
The first step is finding a compatible roommate who can
afford roughly the same amount. (Let's assume that you
are going to live with just one other person; sharing
quarters with two or three roommates can greatly reduce
costs while increasing the potential for conflict.) The second step is finding a place that you both agree on. The
third step is determining just how to share the costs.

David and Mark, who had been roommates at college,
decided to live together when they moved to Philadelphia after graduation. They decided two other things as
well: to split housing costs down the middle, and to flip
a coin for the larger bedroom in the two-bedroom apartment they found. The system worked for David and
Mark, but what about you?

Splitting costs down the middle can generate some
bitterness, to say nothing of hardship, if one earns considerably more than the other. It can also create conflict
if one living space is much larger than the other. You
and your roommate should talk things through in advance
and decide what will work for you. It doesn't have to be
share and share alike. Some alternative solutions: The
person with the larger income gets the larger bedroom—
no coin-flipping allowed—and pays a larger share of the
rent. Or, the person who expects to be at home more
often—perhaps the other travels on business, or spends
many evenings out socializing—pays a larger share of
the utility bill. Perhaps you'll share the utility bill, except
for a proportionate share attributable to one person's air
conditioner. Maybe you'll decide to split grocery costs
for meals you'll eat together, but buy your own food for
meals you'll eat on your own.

Roommate relationships are not nearly as complex as
live-together relationships, because they lack the emotional overlay. But they aren't totally free from anxiety

either. One of the biggest potential problems, and one you may be reluctant to confront at the outset, is what will happen if one of you moves out before the lease expires. You may still be getting along just fine, but David's promotion may take him from Philadelphia to Denver. What happens then? If David's name is the sole name on the lease, you may be without a place to live. If your name is the sole name on the lease, you may be stuck with the entire monthly rent unless you can quickly find someone to take David's place. It may be impossible to know whether one of you will get a job transfer, decide to get married, or simply come to believe that the grass is greener halfway across the country. But you should try to look ahead, and make a rational decision about whether one or both names should be on the lease.

The Dating Game

Old expectations in an era of new rules set the scene for conflict. And there's no bigger mine field than the interaction of male and female singles in the 1980s.

It used to be so easy. He asked her for a date, she waited by the telephone to be asked. He paid for the date, she smiled demurely. He sometimes expected another form of return for his financial investment in an evening's entertainment, she may have been of a different mind. But at least they both knew what game they were playing. Today it's a different game, played by different rules. Neither, very likely, still lives in the parental home. Both, it's virtually certain, earn independent income. *She* may extend the invitation to *him* or they may decide, together, to take in a movie after work. And neither knows, for sure, just who should pay for what.

There are lots of possibilities: He pays; she pays; they split the bill; they take turns paying; they share it in proportion to their income. There are even variations on the possibilities: He pays most of the time, but she buys tickets to an occasional baseball game or little-theater production; she always pays half the bill, but not when it's her birthday or he asks her out to celebrate his raise; she pays for restaurant meals, because she earns more, but he cooks dinner for her at home. This is assuming that the invitation actually constitutes a "date" in the first place rather than two colleagues relaxing together in a convivial fashion. If a meeting continues over lunch or over dinner, it's generally understood that it's still a meeting and the bill is split—or, often, put on the company tab.

It doesn't matter so much who pays for what, in a social setting, as who understands what. Too many promising relationships have broken up over conflicting expectations. If you are extending an invitation, in other words, there's only one way to be sure that the invitee knows that, while you want the pleasure of his or her company, you expect the pleasure to be reciprocal and the costs to be shared. Say so. The question then isn't simply "Would you like to see *A Chorus Line?*" but "Would you like to see *A Chorus Line?* I can pick up tickets for thirty-five dollars apiece if you'll pay your share." If the invitation doesn't specify, then the person on the receiving end may want to make things clear. If the question is vaguely worded—"How about dinner Wednesday night?"—the answer might be "That would be fun, but I don't want to spend more than fifteen dollars; I'm on a tight budget this month."

All this is well and good, you may be thinking, once a relationship has begun. But what happens in the initial stages? Who makes the first move? And how is the other party expected to respond? If we were all liberated, men and women would feel equally free to make the first move, to extend an invitation, to pick up the check. But we're not all liberated and, even if *we* are, we're never quite sure how the other person feels. This leads to some oddly ambiguous situations: She contrives to meet him by the watercooler, just as might have happened in the 1950s, then insists on splitting the bill when he finally asks her to join him for an after-hours drink. He asks her

out to dinner, but won't ask her out again till she recip-
rocates. She wants to ask him out, but fears her "aggres-
sion" will scare him off.

Some women want to play an equal role, in short, and
some men would like them to. This is particularly true
among younger singles, although it's not at all uncommon
among the older crowd—especially when a woman has
been pulling her own weight for some time and can afford
to do so. But some women, and some men, still want to
enact the traditional male-female roles, the scenario in
which he asks and he pays. The problem lies in sorting
out which kind of man and which kind of woman you're
meeting. Will a new friend be pleased or provoked when
you suggest splitting the bill? The only way to be absolutely sure, if you can't tell from the context of your
acquaintance or from other hints that are dropped, is to
ask. It may be awkward. But it's also preferable to otherwise calling an untimely end to what might have been a
beautiful friendship.

Wedding Bills

This heading started out to be "wedding bells" until
my fingers, in a purely Freudian slip, hit the *i* instead.
In fact, when that beautiful friendship turns to thoughts
of matrimony, wedding *bills* may create a conflict you
never contemplated. There may be conflicts between the
bridal couple and their respective parents. Sometimes
there are conflicts between the two sets of parents, which
can last for years to come. And, worst of all, there may
be conflicts between the prospective bride and groom.

The problem is not simply that weddings and their
accompanying festivities can be expensive—the average
wedding, according to the editors of *Modern Bride*, costs
from $4,000 to $5,000; it's easily possible to spend three
times as much. The deeper problem is that the ceremony
and those festivities express cultural and family values.
It can be hard enough to sort out those values if you and
your parents disagree. Add a new set of in-laws to the
equation and sparks can really fly. "John and I wanted

a *small* wedding. But Daddy felt he had to entertain all his clients. We don't even know those people!" Or, "Ginger said she agreed with me, and that the wedding should be small and intimate. Then she let her mother walk all over her and the next thing I knew we had two hundred and fifty guests." But, as Ginger puts it, "My mother only has one daughter. She always dreamed of the kind of wedding she'd make for me. I couldn't let her down, could I?"

Listen to the dialogue. Is Ginger simply playing the role of a loving daughter, knowing how much wedding plans mean to her mother? Does she really, deep down, relish the fairy tale fantasy of a large formal wedding? Or is she stuck in the song-and-dance of childhood, letting her mother use money to control? If Ginger and John really do agree that they want a small wedding, then they must make the point that it is *their* wedding and *their* married lives. And, if it's the only way to make the point, they must be prepared to pay for the wedding themselves.

Many of today's wedding couples do pitch in, sharing the costs with parents if not paying for it all. Many of today's wedding couples are older, with established incomes, and can afford to do so. The average annual household income of the newlywed readers of *Modern Bride* in 1984 was $31,300. They also have established ways, because they are older than the wedding couples of recent decades and are more likely to be emotionally as well as financially independent of parents. Going your own way in planning your wedding reduces the potential for conflict with parents; putting your heads together in planning your wedding today may help to set the scene for your money ways tomorrow.

Money Traps for Singles

When you're living alone, especially as a young single, it's easy to fall into some money traps that can complicate your own life as well as your relationships.

- Overspending, when you're spending for one, is easy to do. But it's a destructive habit. These are the years when, instead of assembling a super wardrobe or the latest electronic gadgets, you should be thinking about your future. With a steadily rising income and no dependents, you're in the perfect position to establish a savings and investment plan that will stand you in good stead in the years ahead whether you marry or not.
- Over-use of credit, to smooth the way for spending, is another temptation. With credit card offers piling up in your mailbox as soon as you land your first job, it's hard to withstand the urge to spend now, pay later. It's particularly hard if you're living alone and feel that you must do nice things for yourself because no one else is doing them for you.
- Relying on parents after you're nominally out of the nest may put you in a double bind, keeping you both financially and emotionally dependent. If you must accept help, try to set the stage so that the help comes without strings. But be selective, in the first place, about when you ask for or accept parental assistance.
- Marking time and refusing to spend money on yourself while you wait to "settle down" may make sense when you're 22 but not when you're 32. Whether you're in your thirties or your fifties, whether or not you hope to marry, you should develop financial know-how and be financially self-sufficient.

· 3 ·

Living Together

CENSUS-TAKERS count more and more single people each year—and more and more of those singles are living together without benefit of matrimony in a relationship that involves more than just being roommates. There were 523,000 unmarried couples living together in 1970 and 1.6 million in 1980, according to the Bureau of the Census, with almost two million by 1985. Most, but by no means all, are young. Almost half have been married before. Twenty-eight percent have children living with them.

Some, especially those who have never been married before, view living together as a prelude to marriage, an extension of courtship. Others believe it is a valid relationship in and of itself, a substitute for marriage rather than a forerunner. Many see living together as neither definitively a prelude to marriage nor a substitute for it, but rather as a temporary connection which may or may not be followed by marriage—to this partner or another. Very often, after a period of living together, one partner or the other urges a more permanent arrangement. If the other agrees, they get married. If not, they are likely to separate.

One way or another, *temporary* is usually the key word in defining the live-together relationship; at least a 1977 study (there aren't many studies of live-togethers) found that the relationship wasn't static; most either got married or broke up within a few years. Couples may get married expecting, or at least hoping, that it will be for a lifetime. Couples seldom set up housekeeping as unmarrieds with any such commitment. "If it works, we'll get married; if it doesn't, we'll split" seems to be the prevailing view. The short-range nature of the relationship, no matter how long it actually lasts, is bound to affect financial management within the household. It also affects the way you each feel about that financial arrangement.

• Don is a widower in his early sixties. Diana is a divorcée in her mid-fifties. They met through mutual friends several years ago, shortly after Don's wife died. They hit it off immediately, and by the time Don sold his house and moved in with Diana, they were virtually living together. Virtually, but not entirely, because each was guarding not only privacy but independence. They still do. "I rewrote my will when Don moved in," Diana says, "because, now that he's sold his house, he'll be left high and dry if anything happens to me. But we still keep everything separate. We still want our children to inherit what we have. And we're still not sure we'll ever get married."

• Erica, an accountant in her early thirties, had never been married when she moved in with Alan, a divorced father of two. They kept finances scrupulously separate at first but, by the time they'd been together for a couple of years, Erica began to feel that separate record-keeping was silly. Alan wasn't so sure. Badly burned by his divorce, he was not at all interested in commingling funds in a new relationship. "If Erica insists on decorating this place instead of simply furnishing it, she can darn well do it herself. I'm not giving her any of my money to mess around with."

• Sally and Glen, on the other hand, didn't even think about financial matters when they took an apartment together after meeting in a management training program. Neither had other obligations. Neither had prior experience to put a damper on this relationship. Nonetheless, they found, money management wasn't easy. "We both earned the same salary, at the beginning," he says, "but I was the only way to save anything and the

only one who had cash to fall back on in an emergency.
She goes through her paycheck like a drunken sailor and
never saves a penny."

If you are a POSSLQ—a "person of the opposite sex
sharing living quarters," in Census Bureau jargon—you
may be young or middle-aged or old. But, most likely,
especially if you are young, you slid into the relationship
without too much planning. It just became easier, as well
as a lot more pleasant, to share one dwelling instead of
commuting between two. It can be a drag, after all, if
you can never remember where you left your favorite
jacket or the book that's due at the library. And why pay
rent on two places if you spend most of your time in
one?

Before you move in, however (or without further delay,
if you're already sharing space), you owe it to yourselves
to size up your financial relationship. Doing so can preclude a lot of hassles, both while you're living together
and if you decide to part. You may not be inclined to
sign a formal agreement—more about contracts later—
but you should, at the very least, sit down and discuss
who will pay for what, who will own what, and to what
extent you will pool your resources. Married couples are
protected both by law and by social custom in terms of
ground rules for the severing of a relationship. Live-
togethers are not.

Live-togethers seem less inclined to fight about money
than married couples—maybe it's simply easier to walk
away and forget the whole thing—but money problems
do rear their familiar heads in even the most informal
relationship. Those problems can be minimized if you
plan ahead, understand your expectations and decide
how you will handle your money.

Setting the Rules

Establishing a financial way of life is complicated, fraught
with emotional pitfalls, for any two individuals setting
up housekeeping together. When those two individuals

are married, however, they are bound together not only by legal rules and social assumptions but also by their own expectations of the relationship. There are, for example, entrenched expectations about sex roles: man the provider and woman the consumer. Even in today's marriages, far more egalitarian than the marriages of our parents, these assumptions seem to hold. Repeated studies have shown that men hold an image of themselves that includes providing for their family. Their wives or partners may work, may indeed contribute in large measure to the family income, but it's the man who feels responsible. And it's the man who assumes the power in decision-making *because* he is the breadwinner.

Many of these expectations are being challenged, and many couples are writing their own rules, but it isn't easy to fully overcome engrained expectations. It isn't easy when you are fully aware of both your own expectations and your partner's, and it's well-nigh impossible when you don't know what the expectations are. The self-assured young lawyer may not realize that she harbors a lingering wish to be protected by the man in her life, just as her mother was protected by her father. The rising executive may fail to recognize that he wants to be nurtured at home. And then there's the daily reality. He lives on credit; she spends cash. She wants a house in the suburbs; he prefers a city apartment. Very few courting couples, no matter how open they are, ever discuss how they feel about money. "After all, it's not very interesting to talk about net worth or projections of income or one's indebtedness," say Philip Blumstein and Pepper Schwartz in their landmark study, *American Couples: Money, Work, Sex,* "so money becomes the last frontier of self-disclosure." This is so, in fact, *"even though each partner may hold strong feelings about how money should be dealt with"* (italics mine).

In the live-together relationship, because it has no long social history and, for that matter, no legal standing (cohabitation is actually still illegal in some jurisdictions), there are fewer entrenched expectations to overcome.

You and your partner can make your own rules, although you will still each bring with you your own emotional baggage of attitudes and assumptions. What you'll do with your money, and how you regard your partner's spending habits, will be firmly rooted in your own emotional past as well as in the practical realities of the present. You may preach egalitarianism, in other words, but practice something quite different. You may insist on financial autonomy, on absolute independence, but still find that one partner wields more power than the other. You may actually talk about your finances more than an about-to-be-married couple—just because you aren't operating on anyone else's set of rules—but you probably won't tackle issues that may arise to haunt you, issues of power, dominance, male-female roles, and your own strong feelings about money. Despite today's large numbers of live-together couples, you're operating in a sociological limbo: as a unit that resembles a married couple but which is actually very different.

Should You Mingle Your Money?

In general, most live-togethers abide by the idea that it's *not* a good idea to mingle their money. Only 9 percent of the live-together couples surveyed by *Working Woman* magazine in 1985 have joint savings accounts; fewer (to my surprise, since checking accounts are a basic money management tool)—only 6.3 percent—have joint checking accounts. Living together is by definition a tenuous arrangement, no matter how many years it may last, and joint accounts are usually a mistake. Not only is it almost impossible to sort out who deposited what into a joint account, but a disgruntled partner can take the money, *all* the money, and run. Should one of you die, and it can happen, even to young people, the other might have great difficulty proving ownership and reclaiming the money. So do as platonic roommates do, and keep money separate while sharing costs. Rent can be divvied down the middle, and the rest split in any agreeable way. One live-together explains that she pays for everything that begins with an "f" sound: food, phone, and garbage. Garbage? Yes, goes the explanation—it's old food.

You might decide with your partner to split the food bills. Or you might pay for food while your partner pays the utility bill. Whatever you decide to do, be sure you both understand what you're doing. And be sure that the bills are paid. It's no fun to have the electricity turned off because one partner thought the other one paid the bill. It's no fun to have endless fights about who is paying for what, or failing to do so. Get your act together. In addition to writing checks of course, there's the cash drain that goes with running a household. One suggestion: a kitchen "kitty," to which you each contribute. "We each put forty-five dollars a month in the kitty," as one woman puts it, "for the days when we run out of detergent or the last lightbulb in the house burns out or we decide to order up a pizza."

All this is easy if your incomes are roughly similar. Very often, however, one partner earns more than the other. That partner is usually, because of the way salaries are structured in our economy, the man. Since both partners are eager to remain independent, cost-sharing under these circumstances must be carefully devised. If you contribute equally to the running of the household, the person who earns less may suffer financially; he or she will almost certainly feel put upon. "I have nothing left over after I put up my share," one woman complains; "he earns much more than I do, so he has lots." If household contributions are proportionate to income, however, the partner who contributes more may feel in a position to make decisions. "I can't afford to buy the theater tickets," as a 28-year-old jewelry designer puts it, "but that doesn't mean I want Mark to pick all the plays." Picking plays is only part of the problem, because Mark is beginning to resent what he sees as a financial burden. While she doesn't want to feel dependent— the essence of living together, for many women, is a sense of independence, and relatively few women in live-together relationships are not employed—the separate pockets inherent in the relationship can create an emotional imbalance. She may actually be economically self-sufficient, but because he earns more he may—unwillingly—feel responsible for her financial support and well-being. If both partners are unhappy about their financial relationship and don't take steps to resolve the problem, that unhappiness is inevitably going to spill over and damage the rest of the relationship.

Unhappiness can be equally vivid when it's the woman who earns the higher income. Among married women, fully 12 percent earn more than their husbands; this income disparity can, as we'll see, adversely affect the relationship. The proportion may be smaller among live-togethers but the feelings can be as intense. She may flaunt her income (at least he sees it that way) by buying things he can't afford. That's the way Chuck saw it when Lee, following a big promotion, bought a VCR. Every movie they watched reminded Chuck of her success. Some women, faced with this kind of reaction, may try to soft-pedal their progress. The problem, however, really isn't that she flaunts affluence but that he feels less successful by comparison.

The problem may be, at least in part, that men and women feel differently about money. "To men it represents identity and power," say sociologists Blumstein and Schwartz; "to women it is security and autonomy." Where these differing values can lead to conflict between husband and wife, live-togethers should, in theory, have the best of all possible worlds. But it doesn't always work out that way. In a live-together relationship, Blumstein and Schwartz go on to say, "The woman chooses autonomy over the security of being supported, and the man chooses the establishment of his own economic identity over the need to control his partner. This should make for a successful financial partnership, as long as the woman is *really* not going to resent the man for rejecting the

provider role, and as long as the man is *really* happy to
live with an independent woman who wants an equal say
in the relationship."

Most married couples do mingle all or most of their
resources. And most married men, as we've seen, expect
(even if they don't relish) financial responsibility. But
whether you're married or not, mingling money or not,
money equals power. With unequal incomes you may
find yourself in a no-win situation even if you do as most
live-togethers do and keep your funds separate. "Cohabitation is a pay-as-you-go system," Blumstein and
Schwartz point out, "and each partner's rights and privileges are based on what he or she contributes." It's hard
to have an equal partnership when financial contributions
aren't equal—and it's hard for contributions to be equal
when incomes aren't.

When you're not married you may have little sense of
responsibility, each for the other. Even so, even as you
are scrupulously guarding your independence, you must
recognize that joining forces emotionally and physically
creates a new entity, a pair that is different from either
of you as individuals. If that pair, that couple, is to survive, financial issues must be considered. Those issues
include your individual attitudes toward money—a couple made of an impulse spender and a saver, married or
not, can have problems. And the issues include, in practical terms, your approach to both household and personal spending.

Whatever you decide to do about household costs,
your own personal expenses, as a rule, will be handled
on an individual basis. You'll take care of your own bus
fare, lunches, cleaning bills, clothing, and the like, and
your partner will do the same. Just be prepared to carry
through. "I had a really hard time asking Jeff for three
dollars when I picked up his pants at the cleaners," Andrea
confesses, "and he never thought to offer. But I finally
decided that it was a matter of him paying his way or of
my not picking up his clothes. We talked about it, and
now we share the costs."

This is one of the emotional dividing lines between
living together and being married. Some married couples
do, in fact, reimburse each other for each pack of ciga-
rettes or dry-cleaning chit. But most don't give it a thought.
Marriage is a joint endeavor, whether there is one income
or two, one bank account or two, but living together is
a form of temporary teamwork.

A lot depends on your expectations. If you intend to
marry, and view living together as a prelude to matrimony, you may start off with separate finances but con-
duct a merger over time. It may indeed be a test of sorts.
If you still divvy up expenses after five years of living
together—you buy the chair and he buys the hassock or
you buy the stereo amplifier and she buys the receiver—
maybe marriage isn't in the cards after all. Blumstein
and Schwartz found in their extensive survey that live-
togethers were more likely to break up when they chose
not to pool their money. Pooling of funds, although it
may not always be a good idea even for married couples,
does indicate an emotional commitment, a feeling that
the relationship will last. But that feeling has to be mutual.
If one of you wants to pool funds and the other does not,
feeling threatened by the very thought, the relationship
may be undermined. It comes down, at least emotionally, to a question of trust. "We do everything together
anyway, and it's just a nuisance writing separate checks,
so I suggested to Dan that we put our money together.
You would have thought I'd suggested a suicide pact.
Judging by his response, Dan thinks I'll run off with his
money."

If you see living together as a valid way of life on its
own, with no wedding bells tinkling softly in the distance,
you'll probably act on that vision and remain independent. Or, if you came to a live-together relationship after
a previous unhappy marriage, you may in fact look toward
marriage but still keep your finances separate. Then again,
you might like nothing better than to marry, but feel
you must stay legally single in order to safeguard your
assets from your partner's first spouse. "That ex-wife of

his would have the court after my earnings in a minute, if I marry Ken," says Alix. "No way will I let that happen." Or, if you're widowed you may stay single in order to protect pensions or trust income from a first marriage, or to limit the taxability of Social Security benefits (currently subject to taxation when total income exceeds $32,000 for a married couple and $25,000 for a single; remaining unmarried gives you an extra $18,000 a year, untaxed). If you're living together in later life you have to come to terms with a number of factors: how you will manage your money and how you will leave that money to your heirs, your own feelings about the situation, and your children's feelings as well.

The practical aspects are all relatively easy to resolve, along with your own feelings (your children's feelings may be another matter) if you both feel the same way *or* if you talk through your differences. Karen finally realized that Dan does love her and does plan to stick around; what she had seen as selfishness and mistrust is a bitter residue of his first marriage. Karen is not alone. In a 1980 study, Graham B. Spanier found that it is more likely for a previously married man to be living with a never-married woman than vice versa. The Karens of this world have a lot of adjusting to do, because attitudes toward money are clearly affected not only by temperament and by early childhood experience but by the experiences of a lifetime.

Marriages may seldom last, these days, till death do us part. But the live-together relationship is, by its very nature, still more tenuous. Married people generally, although not always, share information about income. Live-togethers may keep income details to themselves, on the theory that the partner has no need to know. Again, it depends on your expectations. Some live-togethers claim that they are as emotionally committed to each other as if they were married; all they are missing is a needless piece of paper, a formality. Most recognize, however, that the commitment only goes so far, that there is always the freedom to walk out and be unencumbered. If you are thinking of parting, even if only in the far recesses of your mind, keep your finances separate.

Practical Matters

Keeping your finances separate means separate bank accounts, charge accounts, and property.

Open a small joint bank account purely for household bills, if that will make things easier, but think through your contributions to that account. If your incomes are roughly equal, you may want to contribute an equal sum to the running of the household. If one earns considerably more than the other, however, you may choose to contribute an amount proportionate to each income. One live-in calls this a "Marxist" division. "We split according to our abilities to pay," he says, "which means that I don't have to downgrade my living style to match her income." Just bear in mind the emotional fallout, discussed above, that may develop. And readjust your contributions as circumstances change.

With the exception of a joint household account, if you choose to have one, keep your bank accounts separate. (If you find yourselves still together after a few years, and think you may well be together permanently, you can rethink the matter. At the outset, when things are iffy, separate accounts make the most sense.) If you want your partner to have access to your funds in case of an emergency, William L. Blaine and John Bishop, California attorneys and authors of *Practical Guide for the Unmarried Couple*, have two suggestions: Add your partner's name as an authorized signer on your account, then "keep the bankbook in a place that your partner cannot get to easily"; or, ask your bank to issue your partner a limited power of attorney on your account. If you challenge the odds and open a joint account, one that is larger than a household account, spell out your intentions in a simple agreement. For example: "We have opened account No._____ at _____Bank in both our names. We will both make deposits in and withdrawals from the account. The money belongs to us equally and, on the death of either one of us, will belong to the survivor." Leaving property to an unmarried partner is an issue in itself (see below), and this may or may not work. But you can try.

Credit cards are another danger spot. Sure, you can magnanimously give your partner signing privileges on your American Express or Visa card. And, equally sure, you'll be sorry if you split. (Many of the complications of living together, in a practical sense, are complications arising from splitting up.) Emotionally, you may feel that you should share and share alike. Without the legal benefits conferred by matrimony, however, you are running a risk if you do. A disgruntled partner can break the bank and ruin your credit rating in a single angry buying binge.

What about all the things that you buy with those bank accounts and credit cards? As you set up joint housekeeping, and buy costly items like furniture and electronic gear, it's important to keep track of who buys what and who owns what. The two are not necessarily the same. Suppose you need a couch for your apartment. In order to buy it you might pitch in and make the purchase together. Or one of you could buy it alone. In terms of ownership, however, things are not so simple. Even if the purchase price comes out of one person's pocket, the couch, depending on the circumstances, may belong to you both. When splitting time rolls around, a savvy lawyer could help you reconstruct a conversation that proved, for example, that the only reason *she* paid for the couch in full was that *you* bought all the food and paid the utility bill that month. If the two outlays are roughly parallel, even if one was for durable goods and the other for quickly forgotten consumables, you both may own the durables.

How to avoid such hassles? Hard as it may be, keep track. Start with a log—a simple notebook will do—in which you record your household purchases. Don't bother with the light bulbs, unless you are *both* meticulous record-keepers, or you will create an additional conflict zone. "I can't stand writing everything down, so I 'forget,'" Ilene points out. "Then he gets furious, because he thinks I'm holding out on him." But do list the lamps— and anything else of value that you might each like to claim should the relationship end. (If you *know* that you will never break up, remember that death is another cause of dissolution and death can, sadly, come to the young. If you don't want your partner's family coming in and making off with the swirled glass lamp that you like so much, make a written record of the fact that it belongs to you.) If you're merging two existing households, you'll each have treasured belongings that will clearly belong to one or the other. It's the new things you buy as a couple that may cause problems later on. Just think how vituperative a divorce can be, when formerly loving partners squabble over the spoils. Then think about what can happen when the relationship has no legal standing. You may *think* it's easier to walk away from a live-together relationship than from a marriage. It isn't.

Housing

Many of the issues affecting live-togethers have to do with where they live, especially if instead of taking new quarters one moves in with the other. "I wanted Jeff to move in—he was spending most of his time here anyway—but now I feel as if he's invaded my turf. We're not agreeing on anything, least of all on household spending. He seems to think that because it's my house, and I was paying the bills for it before, I should keep right on paying them now. He's a nonpaying guest, and he won't lift a finger to help. What kind of relationship is this anyway?"

If you move in to your loved one's house or apartment, he or she may well have a proprietary feeling about that space. You, in turn, may feel (consciously or not) that you shouldn't pay for maintenance or improvements on anything you don't own. Such feelings represent a separateness not surprising in a live-together relationship.

But they aren't altogether fair, and they usually generate resentment. "He said he'd help, but his idea of helping is buying bagels for Sunday brunch. That's not *my* idea." You can forestall such misunderstandings by being specific about the arrangements before you get together. Once you're physically sharing space, it's harder, although far from impossible, to discuss how to handle that space. Either way, make sure you establish a set of ground rules that you both can live with comfortably.

If you take new space together, which may be an ideal arrangement because it puts you both on neutral turf, you'll face some other issues. Should both names be on the lease? Should you buy a house together? There are, as always, both practical and psychological factors to consider before you answer. On the practical side, it's easier to qualify for a mortgage or to take an apartment if two incomes bolster the application. This may be why 29.5 percent of the *Working Woman* respondents, live-togethers who by and large did *not* mingle their assets, reported a cosigned mortgage. (Some mortgage lenders, and some landlords, won't consider a second income if the couple isn't married. But at least one lawsuit, in the District of Columbia, has held that unmarried people have the right to have both incomes considered.) On the emotional front, that joint obligation implies a commitment to couplehood. Do you want to make that commitment? Do you *both* want to make that commitment?

If the answer is yes, and especially if you want to buy a house together, be sure to think through all the ramifications. How will you divvy up the down payment, the monthly payments, and the upkeep? What will happen if either of you falls behind in payments? If one of you moves out, will the other have to sell the property? What happens if one partner dies or becomes disabled? Who will be allowed to live in the house? What happens if you no longer want to live together, but you each want to remain in the house? Who owns property within the house, particularly installed property such as built-in cabinets and appliances?

One of the most important questions has to do with the form of ownership itself. There are three forms of joint ownership. One of them, *tenancy by the entirety*, is available only to married couples, because in addition to the right of survivorship it requires joint action; neither partner can independently sell his or her share. As an unmarried couple, you have two choices. *Joint tenancy*, like tenancy by the entirety, has the right of survivorship built in; if one of you dies, the other will automatically receive entire ownership even if there is a will stating otherwise. But joint tenancy does not require joint action; one of you could (at least in theory) sell his or her share without consulting the other. With *tenancy in common*, there is no requirement for joint action and no right of survivorship. You would own the property as business partners; upon the death of one partner, his or her share would be left to the person stated in the will or, if there is no will, to the nearest blood relative as defined by state law.

The form of ownership will be in the deed. But the answers to all the other questions should be put in writing in a separate document. Real estate is a major purchase, and it's vitally important to protect your own and your partner's interest by having a clear and legal agreement. It's also important to make a will, once you've made such a major purchase, so that your interest in the house will go to your partner when you die. Unmarried co-owners may own a house jointly but, in the absence of a will, family can contest the right of the survivor to remain in the house. Don't take that kind of chance.

Wills, Insurance, and Other Weighty Matters

Liz and Evan have been living together for four years, in a comfortably furnished rental apartment they took together and furnished together. Neither, at age 30, has given any thought to writing a will. When I asked Liz what she thought would happen to her property if she were hit by a car, her reaction was quick: "Evan would keep most of it, of course, but I guess I should tell him that I'd like my sister Sue to have my jewelry." Liz is wrong on two counts. Evan would have no right to her property. And sister Sue, whether or not Liz expressed her wishes on the matter to Evan, would have no right to the jewelry. Unless Liz writes a will, legally expressing her wishes in the matter, the laws of her state will dictate who receives her property. Those laws, almost invariably, dictate distribution to the closest blood relatives. So Liz's parents, who have always disapproved of her relationship with Evan, would get the furniture that makes his life comfortable and the jewelry that they may or may not choose to pass on to Sue. If Evan should die without a will, Liz would similarly be out in the cold. Since he has no relatives, however, the property they currently share would be the property of the state.

It isn't easy to contemplate death, at any age, but if you're involved in an extra-legal relationship and you've begun to amass possessions, a will is vitally important. Married people need wills too, because only with a will can you decide who will get your hard-earned property, but at least the state steps in and protects the interests of a surviving spouse. If you've simply been living together, the state will do nothing for you. You're on your own, and you've got to take care of yourselves. Make a will—it isn't expensive to do so. You can always change the beneficiary if you change your minds about the relationship.

Insurance is another issue. If you and your partner are each self-supporting, with no one else financially dependent on either of you (no children from a previous marriage, no aged parents), you probably don't need life insurance. If you buy a house, however, give life insurance some thought. If you would be unable to manage the entire mortgage on your own in the event of your partner's untimely death, life insurance may make it possible. The proceeds of a $100,000 policy, invested at 10 percent, will yield $10,000 a year; that could make the difference between being able to maintain your house and life-style and having to make a drastic change. A $100,000 term life insurance policy is very inexpensive, a matter of a few hundred dollars a year at most for young nonsmokers, and can be well worth the price.

Both wills and life insurance are individual endeavors, and you can write a will or take out a life insurance policy without your partner doing the same. Whether you'll want to do so, though, is open to question. "One of my college friends died in a motorcycle accident several years after graduation and his friend had such an awful time— she was actually locked out of the apartment when the landlord changed the locks, and she couldn't get her own stereo or even her clothes—that I wanted to make a will leaving everything to the man I live with. I figured the will would be a legal document that would prevent that kind of hassle. But *he* wouldn't write a will and I decided not to do one alone. I guess we'll just have to live forever."

Chances are that they'll break up, or get married, before they live forever. But the odds are for a breakup, if their commitment levels are so different. She clearly feels an emotional bond in the relationship that he does not, or that he will not act on, and the disparity does not bode well for the longevity of their relationship.

Splitting Up

George and Elaine lived together for eight years. When they started having problems they consulted a counselor to stave off a breakup. It didn't work, and they separated. But don't let anyone tell you that it's easier to split up if you're not married. It isn't. Not only are there division-of-property ramifications in the wake of the Marvin "palimony" case, there are emotional problems as well. A long-standing relationship is a long-standing relationship, with or without benefit of clergy. And, while living together may make sense for a whole host of reasons, avoiding financial and emotional complications isn't one of them.

The well-publicized 1976 case of Lee Marvin and Michelle Marvin (she legally changed her name to his, on her own, without benefit of matrimony) reverberated throughout the ranks of live-together couples, putting fear in the hearts of men who thought that living together was a way to avoid the financial demands inherent in supporting a wife. Similar cases, some involving celebrities and some ordinary folk, have subsequently held that where a woman has been promised support by a man, she is entitled to that support even if they never married and even if the relationship ends.

But there is one crucial element that seems to unite these cases: The women gave up an independent career or, in the case of the noncelebrities, a simple job, at the men's behest. They fulfilled the homebody role in exchange for support by the live-in lover. Is that your situation? Or are you, like the majority of unmarried couples, secure in your individual capacity to support yourself? If you are financially independent, and if you've kept track of who owns what during your live-together tenure, then you aren't likely to seek "palimony" and you aren't likely to go to court. If you've taken the precaution of signing a contract, in anticipation of breaking up, you'll be ready to pick up the pieces (practically, if not emotionally) and move on.

Contracts: To Sign or Not to Sign

Premarital contracts are all the rage in some circles, and pre–living-together contracts are popular in others. A contract moves beyond verbal assurances of independence and crystallizes your intentions. But it isn't necessarily easy to agree on a contract. "It's so cold and calculating," as one woman put it. "I don't want a business partner; I want a relationship." Another woman felt

differently. A meticulous type, appreciating dotted *i*'s
and crossed *t*'s, she urged her about-to-be-live-in lover
to sign a contract. He refused, saying, "If you have a
contract, you might as well be married," and they broke
up. The problem is that living together, like marriage,
is supposed to be founded on at least some level of affection and commitment. Signing a contract seems, to some
people, to undermine those qualities. "There's no way
I could think of a contract," is the way a New York man
put it, "and at the same time say 'I love you, I want to
spend my life with you.' They are totally, mutually exclu-
sive."

Nonetheless, in this litigious age, contracts do offer a
degree of security. If you can sit down together and
hammer out an agreement, it may mean that you have
a good foundation for a relationship. It should at least
mean that you get your expectations out into the open,
thereby precluding some of the emotional ins and outs
that can arise from miscues.

A contract can be drawn up by a lawyer, but in an
informal live-together relationship where neither of you
intends to make claims on the other and where neither
of you has responsibilities to anyone else, it probably
isn't necessary. You can sit down at the kitchen table,
yellow legal pad in hand, and itemize your points of
agreement. The simplest form of agreement is a waiver
of all financial claims, stating that neither of you has any
intention of sharing income or assets with the other, that
neither partner has any obligation to support the other,
that any property acquired while you live together belongs
to whoever paid for it. Sign it, date it, and put it away.

Contracts can, of course, be longer and more complicated. They are likely to be so if either of you has children
by a previous marriage, has significant assets, or does
intend to provide or accept support. In that case, you
should each see a lawyer (separate lawyers, please) and
work out an agreement that will work for you. Then,
too, once signed, put it away and get on with your life
and with your relationship.

Money Traps for Live-Togethers

Living together is similar to marriage, but very different. It's a state of being all its own, and should be played by its own rules.

- No matter how long you've been cohabiting, don't begin to think you're part of a permanent relationship. Try not to assume provider-dependent roles, either financially or emotionally. Don't merge all your assets. And keep track of who owns what.

- Get your expectations out on the table. It's not necessary to sign a contract—although you may choose to do so—but you should clarify what each brings to the relationship and what each expects to receive.

- Be prepared for change. A casual live-together relationship may gradually move toward marriage. An intense relationship may dissolve. One of you may begin to want commitment, the other may steer clear. A flexible outlook, insofar as possible, helps in coping with change.

· 4 ·

Married Bliss

YOU'VE KNOWN each other for years. Perhaps you've even lived together. Yet, once you're married, you may think you don't know each other at all. Suddenly his little extravagances, the things that made you feel cherished when you were dating, loom larger and look like irresponsibility. Suddenly her reliance on credit, buying now and not worrying at all about paying later, threatens your sense of what's right and proper. Insistence on record-keeping looks like nit-picking, and a wish to save for the future may look like penny-pinching in the present. You accuse her of being a spendthrift; she calls you a tight-wad. What's going on here?

One of the things that's going on is a brand-new array of options for spending coupled with an age-old lack of communication about money. Just look at what you can do with two incomes today, in terms of home furnishings and electronic gear, savings and investment options, vacation travel and retirement plans. But have you talked about what you'll do with your money, other than possibly vague agreement on the notion of owning a house someday? Have you worked out both day-to-day spending patterns and long-range saving? In past decades, sex used to be the primary cause of marital dissension because sex used to be something we didn't talk about. Today we talk about sex. But we still don't talk about money, and money is at the root of much marital conflict. Respondents to study after study agree that money is one of the biggest problems in marriage. *Working Woman* magazine reports in its 1985 survey: "Contemporary couples fight about his spending too much (10 percent), her

53

spending too much (22 percent), what to spend it on (33 percent) and the fact that there is not enough of it to spend (33 percent)."

You may not actually fight over money, although many married people do. But money may be the visible symbol of the adaptive process that takes place as two individuals become a couple. Resolving differences about money, which in fact may be differences about values and priorities, is a way of working out your new relationship. That's because each of you brings with you a set of internal expectations about marriage, expectations which may never have been expressed. Inside, you may anticipate re-creating your parents' marriage...but you may never have told your partner, because you haven't verbalized it yourself, that this is what you expect.

That's what happened with Jane and Noel. "I give her thirty-five dollars for subway and food, out of the money she earns and turns over to me. If she wants anything else, she comes to me and asks and I give her the money. Sometimes she complains but basically we agree, because we both want to control our spending and save money. Anyway," Noel continues, "that's the way my father did it—only I remember him standing in the corner with his back to my mother every time he had to give her money. She never even knew how much money he had in his hand. Jane knows how much we have." But that doen't mean that Jane is happy. Such doling out of money is archaic, a relic of days when wives were supposed to be ignorant of financial affairs. Jane accepted the situation initially, partly because Noel wanted it that way and partly because it echoed her own family background, but resentment is beginning to surface. This is a clear case where old role models won't do. Jane and Noel should discuss their mutual goals and work out a new way of handling their money.

Parental models also haunted Kevin and Diane. They never discussed money before marriage, but if they had, they would never have anticipated any conflict. After all, they came from virtually identical backgrounds where both fathers were breadwinners and both mothers were homemakers. But Kevin's father turned over his weekly paycheck and his mother paid all the bills, balanced the accounts, and made most of the spending decisions. Diane's parents worked on a different set of principles: Her father doled out weekly allowances to both wife and children and made all the major spending decisions himself. The result: Kevin expects Diane to make her own decisions. She, instinctively, consults him before she buys more than groceries. He doesn't understand why she does, and she doesn't understand why he gets irritated. Left unchecked, that irritation may grow and begin to fester, eating away at the core of the marriage, unless Kevin and Diane explore their differing attitudes.

Even if you've lived together for years, marriage is different. When you live together, because it's an unorthodox arrangement, you make your own rules. You tend to keep your money separate, with no need to account to the other about spending. You each pay your own way, splitting household costs. You don't have to know that she spends $30 a week on her hair or he spends as much on tennis lessons, and if you do know you don't care. Once you're married, however, the picture changes. Unless you sit down and consciously decide how you'll handle money as a couple, you may find yourself bound by the unwritten rules of marriage. According to those rules, everything goes into a common pot. That's nice, in many ways. "The big step for us was paying the phone bill jointly," one young husband notes. "Before, we figured out exactly who made which calls and we divided the bill. Now we're a unit." When you play by those rules, though, especially if you haven't really thought through whether they apply, you may well find yourself arguing over who spends how much for what. Telephone calls, hair care, tennis lessons, car accessories . . . almost anything valued by one partner and scorned by the other can be cause for conflict.

The arguments may have little to do with money and more to do with personality. Rob is a squirreler. Never quite confident about the future, he finds it hard to let loose and spend in the present. His wife's mind-set is different. "I see us as two people with good incomes and potential for better. Why shouldn't we enjoy what we have?"

Family background, also significant, may be easier to identify as a source of differences. If one of you comes from an economically secure, free-spending family and the other from parents worried about too much month for the money, you may have fundamentally different attitudes toward spending. "When Alice nagged me about spending too much I felt like a little boy again, unable ever to spend." Nagging about cutting costs was not productive; nagging seldom is. This couple was deeply in debt before the husband realized that he could cut back on spending and not feel deprived. Over time, free spenders and savers often move closer together. He (or, sometimes, she) begins to cut back on spontaneous spending; she (or, sometimes, he) becomes able to spend more freely.

But personality and family background pale behind the dominant theme: Money is power, both factually and symbolically. If you earn more than your spouse, you may feel empowered to make decisions. If you earn less, you may feel you must ask "permission" to spend over a mentally designated limit. If you have no money in your own name, you must ask your spouse for every penny. The spouse distributing the largesse feels powerful. The asking spouse feels like a child. This can be the situation with a nonearning spouse, whether a wife or a husband, if the earning spouse retains total control of the pursestrings. And it can happen even where there are two incomes if, for instance, husband and wife have agreed to bank her salary and live on his. In Rita's case, as she explains, "My salary seemed to become invisible once it was banked. Before I knew it, he had taken over our joint account, doling out money to me only if he approved of what I wanted to buy. It was humiliating."

Such exercise of power, by either spouse, may lead to

manipulative games. Rita, feeling humiliated by her husband's control of the purse strings, makes him feel guilty for depriving her of the tennis club membership she "needs" to wind down after work. Tom, his heart set on a telescope that his wife thinks is extravagant, charges half the purchase price and pays for the rest in cash, thereby getting (she thinks) a "bargain." The games are endless, but they may also be destructive, because married adults really shouldn't treat each other like children.

One income or two, each of you is entitled to some discretionary money of your own. There's no reason in the world why one adult has to consult another about spending money on personal pleasure . . . just so long as that personal pleasure doesn't undermine economic security for the couple as a unit. But many people, caught up in stereotypical role models, find it hard to act within a couple as independent adults. *He* thinks, if just subconsciously, that as the "man of the house" he is obligated to be the provider and to make family decisions. *She* thinks, also subconsciously, that it's right and proper to defer to her husband. Such a mutual agreement, spoken or (more likely) unspoken, may even work well for the couple, unless and until one of them decides it will no longer fly. Then, if it's the wife who wants equal rights and the husband who wants to retain male dominance, the power struggle can shift into high gear. "Fred grumbled when I bought a suit without asking him, even though I'm earning my own money and even though he buys his clothes without consulting me. He had a fullfledged tantrum when I bought a coat. Yet he had the gall to 'surprise' me with an expensive couch after we agreed to pick out furniture together."

If you start out together as newlyweds, with two incomes and shared decision-making, then you'll be less likely to run into the money-as-ego routine. But there may still be snags. Most young women today expect to earn (although they may also take time off) and expect to be equal partners in marriage (although they may also enjoy feeling protected and provided for). Most young men today expect their wives to work (it's the new norm), want them to work (it relieves the enormous burden of being the sole support), and expect to share in decision-making (up to a point, where traditional role-model expectations sometimes take over in the most liberated male). Older men, as we'll see in Chapter 8, are more likely to be threatened, because a wife's return to work after years at home constitutes a change in the status quo. But couples of any age can be confronted by money-as-power routines, as one partner or the other attempts to exert dominance over the other.

Power plays can revolve not only about money itself but around such issues as whose career takes precedence and who cares for the house. For many couples, whatever the issue, it's a matter of the higher-earning partner being dominant. For years this meant that a wife would willingly (or unwillingly) give up her career, if necessary, to follow her husband to another city. For years it meant that the primary household responsibility, no matter who worked how many hours, belonged to the wife. Today, ever so slowly, things are changing. Most men still earn more than most women (although fully 12 percent of all women earn more than their husbands; see Chapter 8). But even where men do earn more, women's careers are seen as important. Even where men earn more, house-hold chores are more likely to be seen as a shared respon-sibility.

New Rules

Marriage is traditional, yet marriage has changed. We reenact the scripts of our parents. Yet we also find our-selves writing new rules, creating new structures of mar-riage, because:

• The average age of first marriage, as noted earlier, is just about as old as it's ever been. If you're in your mid-twenties or older when you marry, you're a different person from the bride or groom who moves directly from the parental home to the marital home. You earn your own income and have been earning it long enough so that you've decided how best to spend and save it. You've developed your own patterns for coping with the world in general and with money in particular. You are likely to be, in a word, both financially and emotionally independent. As a man, if you're financially and emotionally independent, you're less likely to have your ego tied up with either how much money you make or whether you control that money in the family. As a woman, if you're financially and emotionally independent, you're used to earning your own income and being autonomous, in control of your own decisions.

• Expectations of appropriate role models have changed. Man-the-breadwinner and woman-the-homemaker are no longer automatic roles assumed with marriage. Both probably earn incomes, both probably share household tasks, both expect to share in spending decisions. The baby boom generation, defined in numerous studies as those born between 1946 and 1964, is committed to work, typically claims that the "head-of-household" role is shared, and in fact does share most spending and shopping decisions.

• Ego, status, and self-esteem are all wrapped up with earning money and, today, *both* partners in a new marriage usually earn money. Wage-earning by the wife is no longer considered a threat to the husband, as it was right through the 1960s; see, for example, the 1968 edition of a book called *The Young Marriage*. But two-career couples must nonetheless accommodate to each other's status needs if the marriage is to work. That takes a degree of compromise, negotiation and, above all, communication. These are skills that can be learned (see p. 78).

New roles frequently clash with old expectations. Power and decision-making have traditionally been highly structured along male-female lines. Today, according to Oliver Bjorksten and Thomas J. Stewart of the Medical University of South Carolina, writing in *Marriage and Divorce: A Contemporary Perspective*, they are "distributed more reciprocally in the typical dual-breadwinner home." Couples may agree on equal decision-making power, but real change is slow, with a resulting strain on "liberated" marriages despite rational agreement on issues. The less predictable our roles, in other words, the more anxiety we feel.

The Ties That Bind

Our parents, by and large, played by different rules. Their attitudes and expectations, despite our best efforts, often linger on. Freud pointed to the multiple occupants of the marriage bed, referring to parents' influence on sexual development and behavior. Power plays involving money are also occasionally more than two-sided, as parents get into the fray, either through past influence or present interference. Young marrieds, just as much as young singles, may have trouble severing the apron strings. Sometimes it's her parents who hover, offering help; sometimes it's his. Sometimes he's willing to accept help and she is not; sometimes it's the other way around. Sometimes they agree that they could use a hand, and find parents refusing.

If you and your spouse disagree about accepting help, the simplest rule is: Don't. Accepting monetary help over your partner's objections may drive a wedge between you; in the worst case, the wedge may be permanent. "Irene ran to Daddy every time she wanted something we couldn't afford," says a recently divorced 28-year-old man. "She refused to wait for anything, or to give us a chance."

Even if you and your spouse agree on the issue of parental subsidy, you're treading on an emotional mine field. It's hard for parents to relinquish habits of dominance over children; wielding the purse strings reinforces the dominance. "Jim had an emergency appendectomy when we were first married. I was still in grad school, he was new on the job, and we didn't have health insurance. I appreciated my in-laws' help. But not for long. Giving that help seemed to make them

think they could take over, speaking to his doctor and
elbowing me out of the way. Never again!" Or, "Nell's
parents said they would stake her to law school. That
was fine—until it turned out that, in return, we were
supposed to visit every Sunday. They never said that
was the quid pro quo, but they were 'terribly hurt, after
all we've done for you' if we made other plans." Unless
you're sure that no strings are attached, it might be best
to neither ask for nor accept parental help—at least until
you've firmly established your independence as a married couple.

Yours, Mine, Ours

If you and your spouse are embarking on a first marriage, it's virtually certain that you both will be working
outside the home and that you will continue to do so, at
least until a first child is born. Because you're both earning an income, however, doesn't necessarily mean that
you will have an egalitarian marriage. There are many
styles of marriage. Which one you'll have at the outset,
and which one you may adopt as the years go by, depends
on your individual expectations and on how well they
mesh.

Because money is an instrument of power, the marriage style you adopt may depend at least in part on who
earns how much. But even when you earn roughly similar
amounts, psychological factors may determine your marriage style. Caroline Bird, in *The Two-Paycheck Marriage*, describes several variations:

• "Pin money" couples play down the wife's financial
contribution in the interests of a traditionalist form of
male supremacy. This attitude is more common among
older couples where a wife is returning to the work force
than it is among young couples who start out on a two-
career footing, but it can crop up wherever a couple is
most comfortable with the traditional provider-dependent roles. It's also likely where a husband feels threat-

ened in his role as provider by his wife's earnings. "Pin
money" couples tend to live on the husband's income,
putting the wife's into savings or into whatever luxuries
she wants to acquire. The idea, if not the reality, is that
her income isn't really necessary. (But there may come
a time when "pin-money" husbands protest. As one put
it, "*My* money is always *our* money; why should *her*
money be *her* money?")

• "Earmarker" couples are what Bird calls "neo-tra-
ditionalists." They deal with the threat of a wife's income
by setting it aside for specific goals such as a down payment on a house or a special vacation. "I'll work until
we start a family," says one young woman. "But we're
trying not to spend any of my income, because we know
we'll need it later."

• "Pooler" couples put all their money together,
thereby losing sight of who earned what, but they don't
necessarily have equal say in spending decisions. Most
couples pool their money. "It's a sign of trust and that's
what marriage is all about." But most couples also consist
of a senior partner, who can make unilateral spending
decisions, and a junior partner, who defers to the senior.
The senior partner is usually, although not always, the
husband.

• "Bargainer" couples are the true radicals, and are
relatively rare. With separate accounts for individual
earnings, they scrupulously divide both income and outgo
much as live-togethers do. While this practice maintains
individual independence, it can also be seen as less than
full commitment to marriage. Keeping assets in your own
name may prove very helpful if you ever divorce...but
keeping assets in your own name may appear to be a
prelude to divorce.

Should Money Be Pooled?

Keeping separate accounts minimizes some conflicts
over money. If you don't know what your spouse is
spending, and on what, you're less likely to object. At

the same time, keeping separate accounts is seen by many couples as a threat to the very concept of marriage.

You'll probably pool your funds, as most young couples do. But that doesn't necessarily mean that each and every penny must be commingled. There are a variety of ways to accomplish pooling. Erika and Joe, for example, decided to establish a joint account purely for household bills and to have individual accounts for everything else. But one month Joe didn't have enough money in his account for the car payment, so Erika paid it from her account. Then Erika needed a new winter coat but was short of cash when the Election Day coat sales were on; Joe helped her out. It began to seem silly to balance three checking account statements each month, and they put everything together in a single joint account.

Deirdre and Ed took the opposite course. They started out three years ago with a joint household account. But they ran into trouble, partly because her income is three times as large as his but primarily because he's a poor money manager. "He drove me crazy," Deirdre recalls, "writing checks and never entering them. And I'm the only one who ever cared about balancing the account." So they went to separate accounts. He pays the monthly maintenance on their co-op apartment as well as his own personal expenses. She pays everything else. The system works just fine.

You have choices too: You might have a small joint household account, à la Erika and Joe, with separate accounts for everything else. It may be cumbersome— there's that balancing of three accounts each month— but it does eliminate some hassles about spending. Just be sure that you communicate enough so that (a) you have enough money to pay essential bills and (b) you save a portion of your income. Or you might put almost all your money into one joint account, reserving some "mad money" in small separate accounts. With this system, you operate jointly as a family unit yet have some money on hand to buy your spouse a present or yourself something frivolous. Or you might not pool at all, instead keeping totally separate accounts and a careful budget so that all bills are handled via one account or the other. And, as a last choice, one I don't recommend, you might put everything together and keep nothing separate at all. Investment adviser Laura Sloate agrees. As she put it in a *Vogue* interview, "It's fine to spend money pooled but not to keep it pooled...because of the divorce rate, for reasons of independence and security. It leaves the couple with greater flexibility in the future if their money isn't pooled."

It's hard to be so clear-sighted in the throes of romance. Nonetheless, I suggest one of the first two approaches, with some money pooled and some kept separate, in a proportion that suits you both. Remember: While pooling funds does indicate the trust that is fundamental to marriage, pooling everything frequently precludes independence. At least it may do so for one partner. The partner with the larger income, typically the husband, may spend as he pleases. The partner with the lower income, typically the wife, will consult with him before spending. "I think that's where not having separate money can become very destructive," says Pepper Schwartz; "you don't have the dignity of your own decision-making."

It's not surprising that Blumstein and Schwartz found in their study, reported in *American Couples*, that wives are often less willing to pool all their money than husbands. It comes down to who wields the power. "A wife usually has a smaller income than her husband, and if pooling occurs, her money gets lost in the larger pot and gets called 'ours'—and she loses control over it. The ability to have her own separate account gives the wife more autonomy."

Anne Seifert, author of *His, Mine and Ours*, discovered this for herself and went to the opposite extreme. Starting marriage with pooled resources and a joint account, "we discussed endlessly how the money should be spent. I wanted to make long-distance phone calls. He said it was a waste of money. I had always used the

phone freely and was annoyed by his criticism. He bought
a motorcycle. I said if he bought a motorcycle, then I
should be able to make long-distance phone calls. After
all, it was *our* money." Before the arguments got out of
hand, they found a solution, what Seifert calls the "Separate Property System." Such a system entails, as you
might guess, scrupulously separate accounts plus the
labeling of joint and personal purchases. A joint purchase
is one you'll both want and use; a personal purchase is
something for yourself alone.

Under the Seifert system, personal purchases need
not be discussed. Joint purchases are discussed and
recorded, so that you'll know who paid for what and can
settle up at the end of the month. Then, if you've agreed
on a joint purchase but not on how much you're each
willing to spend, you can pay disproportionate amounts
out of your separate accounts. It entails a lot of bookkeeping, but some couples may want to give it a try. It
also entails a very dispassionate view of marriage, and
may be as destructive to a relationship as totally pooled
assets. "Having separate accounts becomes destructive
when there is no community," Dr. Schwartz notes,
"nothing you share in common and therefore no sense
of future and risk together."

Ideally, therefore, some income and assets should be
pooled, others kept separate—how much of each depends
on how much you have (the more you accumulate, the
better off you are likely to be with individual ownership;
see p. 72) and your own comfort level. If you're a wife
who has kept her own name in marriage, this kind of
bookkeeping, with separate accounts and separate credit,
may make sense for you. If you are perfectly willing to
trade your name for his you might still, looking ahead
to the divorce stories of Chapter 5, keep at least some
assets in your own name.

If you're just starting out, you have the perfect opportunity to structure accounts as you please, to elect autonomy if you choose. Even if you've been married for a
while, however, it's still possible to restructure accounts.

In fact, you should expect that your money management techniques will change as you grow both as individuals and as a couple.

The Family Financial Officer

If you keep completely separate accounts, you will each be responsible for your own financial management. If you fail to record checks or to balance your checkbook, you'll be the one to suffer. (Of course, if you consistently run out of funds and fail to define mutual goals, your marriage may suffer as well.)

If you pool your funds, as most couples do, you'll probably share in decision-making. That doesn't mean, however, that you'll share in all the mundane daily tasks that go with money management. One of you will probably function as the "family financial officer," responsible for record-keeping. Neither of you will probably elect the job but one of you, preferably the one who's better at it, will have to take it on. "We thought we should do *everything* together, when we first got married," says a woman who's been married for four years. "But it just didn't work to have both of us trying to do the paperwork. So we thought we'd take turns; I'd balance the checkbook one month and Chuck would do it the next. But Chuck never seemed to get around to it, so guess who's stuck with the job."

After much trial and error, bucking different temperaments and styles, another couple worked out a different arrangement. Bills are gathered, with due dates noted on a calendar. Then, on two Sundays a month, they sit down together and one writes the checks while the other stuffs them in the envelopes. "This is the only method we could find that lets us both know exactly what's going on."

Again, the best arrangement is a workable arrangement, one that works for you. In most households, even among traditional couples where the man makes the larger financial decisions, it's the woman who handles the tedi-

ous paperwork. I'd like to suggest something a little bit
different: Both of you, together, should determine mutual
goals and chart a financial path to meet those goals. One
of you, just for ease of operations, should handle financial
maintenance. But both of you should know how to do
so. Once a year, for a couple of months at a time, the
nonmanagerial partner should take over. Just writing the
checks, recording them, and balancing the checkbook
give such a clear sense of what's happening in your financial life that you both should have the opportunity to do
so.

Getting started also entails mastering some financial
facts of life:

• *Setting goals and objectives* comes first. Goals are
an expression of your mutual values, a long-range look
at what's most important to you both. What is your financial destination? Enough money to buy a house? to quit
work and go skiing? to travel around the world? to start
your own business? to have a baby and take a couple of
years at home? You may each have separate individual
goals as well, but your major long-term financial goals
should be mutual. Once you've clarified long-term goals,
recognizing that they may take years to reach, you can
develop objectives that will move you toward each goal.
For example: Saying you want to buy a house is com-
mendable but vague. Figuring out specific investments
that will enable you to buy a house is much more productive. Incidentally, the very exercise of sitting down
and clarifying your goals and then working out objectives
to meet the goals will be useful. Some couples don't
tackle this exercise until much later in their married
lives, with some rude surprises. "I was stashing away
every penny so that I could quit my job with a computer
manufacturer and go into business as a computer consultant. I thought Rick supported the idea—until he
came home with brochures for a trip to New Guinea he
said we couldn't pass up. If we take that trip, it will put
me back at least a year."

As an independent young couple, you don't *have* to

strive for the same goals at the same time. But you do have to get your act together, and make sure you understand where your partner is heading. Otherwise, misplaced expectations can undermine your marriage.

• The very thought of *budgeting* makes many people cringe, yet working out some sort of budget is the best way to make your financial dreams come true. Some people learn this the hard way. "We never sat down to figure out what we actually had. We just figured, I guess, that we were both earning such good incomes and working so hard to do it that we were entitled to as much fun as we wanted. So we never cooked; we ate out all the time. We went to Vermont to ski for a week last January and then, in March, got so tired of winter we went to the Caribbean for a week. By the time we'd been married a year and a half, we were $8,000 in debt."

Budgeting, if you can bring yourself to do it, can prevent such a catastrophe. And it needn't be painful. It will take a few hours to get organized on the first go-round, but a monthly half hour should do the trick thereafter. Start by sitting down, together, and writing down your monthly income. Include take-home pay plus other regular sources of income, such as dividends and interest, but don't count overtime or bonuses; they may be here today and gone tomorrow. Then list your fixed expenses (housing, transportation, insurance, etc.) and your flexible costs (food, clothing, entertainment, etc.). If you're paying for separate expenses out of separate accounts, this is the time to determine who pays for what; your periodic review can keep the split equitable.

• Be sure to include *savings* in your calculation, and work out, together, how you will handle those savings. Start by amassing two to three months' income in a liquid form of savings, something like a bank account or money market fund that you can get at easily in case the car needs a major overhaul or one of you is laid off. Then design a savings/investment plan to meet your long-term goals. If your primary goal is a house, for example, work out which portion of each income should be invested for

that purpose and pick investments that will work for you.
If you're both timid about financial risk, think about
certificates of deposit or government securities as temporary parking places for your down-payment capital;
pick maturity dates roughly in line with your projected
purchase date. If you're not sure when you'll be ready
to buy a house, make your purchases with staggered
maturity dates so that you can keep rolling the money
into new fixed-term issues. If you're willing to take some
risk in the interest of possible capital appreciation, think
about common stock; just remember that the market may
be down when you're ready to sell, and you could sustain
a loss.

And what if, as so often happens, you're of totally
opposite temperaments? Women are frequently, although
of course not always, of a conservative mind when it
comes to investing. When women have equal or chief
say in investment decisions, *Working Woman* found in
its 1984 survey, those investments tend to be in risk-
free instruments such as certificates of deposit. Men are
more likely to take risks. Where do you stand? And how
do you reconcile your differences? One solution—a good
idea in any case—is diversification. If you balance your
investments among the conservative and the speculative,
taking major risks only with money you can afford to
lose, you'll avoid the broken dreams that can result from
putting all your nest egg in one basket. Another possibility: Diversify your *family* portfolio via *individual*
investments. Alternate your investments, with roughly
equivalent sums, in investment vehicles that make you
each comfortable. Keep a written record, but don't discuss your investments if they'll make your partner fran-
tic. "Buying the over-the-counter stock of a brand new
software company seemed to me about as sound an
investment as playing the slots. I finally told Fred that
the only way we could handle his taking a speculative
fling is if I don't know about it *and* if he doesn't gamble
the rent money."

While some investment advisers suggest that two-income couples with no dependents can afford to take major risks in the interests of capital growth, unlike older folk with sizable family responsibilities, I suggest a more cautious tack. Yes, if you have discretionary funds, by all means consider speculative stocks or a real estate limited partnership for a portion of your portfolio. But remember, too, that you probably will have more responsibilities later on coupled with a slower rate of income growth. These are the years to build a financial foundation for those later years. And you don't build a foundation without being a little bit careful. So take some risks, if you're of a mind to do so, but balance those risks with conservative investments like certificates of deposit, government securities, solid mutual funds and blue chip stocks. The sheer power of compounding over time lends tremendous weight to conservative investments made at an early age.

• *Credit* is a handy-dandy tool for today's money managers, but here, too, it's possible to run into problems. There's the problem that results from mutual disregard of credit limits, the kind of nonthinking behavior that results in running up an $8,000 debt in a year and a half of marriage. And there's the kind of problem that stems from one spouse being credit-happy and the other preferring to pay with cash. "It wasn't just that I was spendthrift, in Frank's book, when he found out about the bills. It was that I didn't love him, that I was trying to prove I was an Amazon. All kinds of ugly things came out." Frank may indeed have been terrified at out-of-control bills, even if those bills were in Amy's name and paid from Amy's bank account. His frugal nature just couldn't accept careless spending by his wife, even if the money was her own. If *you* have different attitudes toward credit, assuming that you can afford to pay the bills you incur (if you can't, don't charge), work out those attitudes during one of your goal-setting sessions. If you approach the issue objectively, on a dollars-and-cents basis, you should be able to reconcile your differences.

Whether your credit attitudes are similar or different, however, you should each maintain credit in your own name (not Mrs. John Jones, if you're a woman, but Mary Jones). This is still more of a problem for women than for men. But you can legally change your name at marriage, if you choose to do so, and still maintain your own credit rating. Just notify your credit grantors, each store and bank, that you have married, have such-and-such a name, but are maintaining your separate credit identity. If you open new accounts, you're entitled to have them be individual accounts as long as you are earning an income of your own. If you are not earning an income, you can open joint accounts with your husband (you can do so anyway, if you wish) and ask that a credit record on the account be maintained in each of your names. This will ensure that you do not become a "nonperson" in the credit world.

• *Insurance* seldom sparks much conflict (unless you disagree on what to carry and how much), but it should be considered as part of your financial setting-up-housekeeping. There are three types to consider: life, health, and property. As a two-income couple with no dependents, you probably don't need life insurance. But there are exceptions. If one of you has dependent parents, life insurance might be appropriate. Or, if you've made a major expenditure (a condominium, for example) contingent on both incomes, life insurance might also be appropriate. Otherwise, as long as each of you could be self-supporting and not financially strapped without the other, forget it.

Your health insurance needs are probably met through your on-the-job benefit programs. You should check, however, to see just what coverage each of you has and what benefits might overlap. If you contribute toward the cost of the group plan and you do have overlapping benefits, it might make sense to drop the less inclusive policy (you usually can't collect under both policies anyway) and put the money toward catastrophic coverage.

Such a policy, with a large deductible which could be equivalent to the maximum payment under the basic group plan, would pay for long-term or catastrophic illness. The other form of health insurance, one you should absolutely not be without, is disability income insurance which would replace a portion of your income if you are ill or injured. If you don't have disability insurance through your job, you can take an individual policy on your own. You can keep costs down by electing a ninety-day waiting period before benefits begin (your bank account or money market fund should cover that period of time), but do have benefits continue at least until age 65.

Property insurance protects against financial loss if your personal property is stolen or damaged, and against personal liability if someone is injured on your premises. If you own a house or condominium you probably have insurance; if you live in an apartment you should have insurance as well. In the event of an apartment fire, your landlord's policy would pay the landlord for damage to the premises; it would not pay you for damage to your personal belongings.

As You Amass Property

At the beginning of your married life, when it's a first marriage for both, chances are that you don't own very much property. What you *do* own, the property that you bring into marriage, will remain in individual ownership—unless you mingle it with property belonging to your spouse. Pool your individual bank accounts into a single joint account, for example, and neither of you will have individual title.

But what about property you acquire together? How should this property be owned? You may assume that the things you work together to buy are things that belong to you both. This is not necessarily the case. It depends on the law in your state and on how you record ownership.

In the eight community property states (Arizona, California, Idaho, Louisiana, Nevada, New Mexico, Texas, and Washington) and in states that have adopted what's called a "uniform marital property law" (just Wisconsin, at this writing, although it's under consideration in other states), property acquired during marriage is assumed to be owned fifty-fifty by husband and wife. In other states, ownership is up for grabs.

Uniform Marital Property

The traditional Church of England marriage ceremony contains the vow "with my worldly goods I thee endow," Mary Moers Wenig, professor at the University of Bridgeport School of Law, wrote in 1983 in *Women's Law Journal*, yet at the ceremony uniting Prince Charles and Princess Diana in 1981, the Prince instead said "All my goods, with thee I *share*." The concept of sharing property acquired during marriage, rooted in the revolutionary changes in the legal status of women in the last decades, is what the Uniform Marital Property Act is all about. Although it's only been adopted in one state thus far, it has had and will continue to have a far-reaching impact on marriage everywhere by bringing consistency to what has been wild inconsistency in the laws of the various states.

The Uniform Marital Property Act is similar to community property in recognizing that property acquired during marriage, by the efforts of either spouse, is shared property owned by both spouses. It is different from community property in that management and control of the property is up to the marriage partners. It will be possible, in other words, to have your name on an asset so that you can manage that asset and yet have it legally belong to both you and your spouse. The act has a lot of leeway, permitting married couples to reach their own agreement about the management of property. At the same time, it protects the interests of both partners. (Not everyone agrees with this approach. As a representative of the National Organization for Women said at a Washington hearing on the Uniform Marital Property Act, "Many women have been socialized to believe that any show of lack of trust in their husbands indicates they don't love them." Many women would therefore be reluctant to insist that their names be put on titles and would as a result be left with "all the burdens of ownership and not the benefits of control.")

For today's partnership marriages, however, movement toward the Uniform Marital Property Act is a movement toward recognition that marriage is an economic partnership as well as a social one. If state law is going to intrude into the marriage partnership at divorce and at death, as it has always done, then perhaps it is in our interests to have state law explicitly provide that we own marital property jointly with our spouses and that we, as a partnership, may arrange how those assets are to be managed.

Pros and Cons of Joint Ownership

In the so-called "common law" states, where title indicates ownership, equitable distribution laws have given both spouses some claim on marital property. But equitable distribution applies only at divorce. What should you do about property ownership while you are happily married? If you're starry-eyed and in love, you may assume that joint ownership is the way it ought to be. But, as already discussed with respect to bank and charge accounts, it's not that simple.

There are advantages to joint ownership:
- Jointly owned assets bypass probate proceedings and go directly to the surviving spouse when the first spouse dies, saving both time and expense.
- Jointly owned assets are available to both spouses, to use as needed. Household bills may be paid by either of you, with a joint bank account, and money may be withdrawn in case of emergency.

- Jointly owned assets are controlled by both partners, not by one alone.
- Joint ownership, like the pooling of funds, implies a commitment to the marriage.

There are also disadvantages:

- Jointly owned assets (and individually owned assets, too, in some states) are subject to "equitable distribution" in divorce, which may not mean distribution according to who contributed what. (This can be an advantage to the spouse whose name would not otherwise be listed as an owner, a disadvantage to the other.)
- Jointly owned assets may not be left to anyone else in your will; they are already designated as the property of the surviving spouse.
- Jointly held bank accounts may, in some states, be completely cleaned out by one partner without the knowledge of the other.
- Other jointly held property may be frozen if both owners fail to act. If one owner is away on business or incapacitated or simply stubborn, the other may be unble to dispose of securities or real estate because two signatures are required. If you should divorce, your jointly owned property may be frozen until negotiations are complete—unless you both, as joint owners, agree to the sale. If one dies, jointly owned property may be frozen until taxing authorities complete their investigation.
- Joint accounts also mean joint accountability: One of you can undermine the credit rating of the other; both of you can be in jeopardy if one of you is sued.

Joint ownership no longer saves on estate taxes, because current tax law permits unlimited amounts to be left to a spouse without any estate tax being due. Joint ownership may, however, have income tax implications if property has appreciated in value. As the Research Institute of America points out, only half of jointly owned property is valued for tax purposes as of the date of one spouse's death; the other half is valued as of the purchase date. For example: If you inherit a jointly owned house that cost $50,000 at purchase and is now worth $100,000, your inherited share will have a "cost basis" for tax purposes of $50,000 (half the current value) and the already owned share has a cost basis of $25,000 (half the original purchase price). The new cost basis for the entire house becomes $75,000 and, if you later sell the house for $150,000, you might well owe capital gains tax on the $75,000 difference. The Uniform Marital Property Act, if passed, would establish the entire value of the jointly owned property as of the time of death, thereby eliminating or reducing the tax. Meanwhile, in the absence of the law, many professional advisers suggest that such taxes can be avoided by putting ownership of valuable assets in the name of the spouse most likely to die first. I don't know how you can tell which one that is, even when you are in your seventies; you certainly can't make such a guess, barring serious illness, when you are the age of most newlyweds.

Joint ownership, in another Catch-22 situation, eliminates creditors' claims at death but can be a problem during life. If you own property jointly, it may be assessed for debts due by either of you. It's particularly important, therefore, to keep the name of a business-owning spouse off any joint property. If you run a business and go into debt, and your husband's name is on your house along with your own, your creditors could attach the house. In this case, you'd be better off letting your husband have sole title to the house.

Clearly there is no easy answer to the ownership riddle. You may decide that some property should be owned individually and some jointly. Before you decide, and just to complicate matters further, here's a rundown of three types of joint ownership:

Tenancy by the entirety, permitted only between spouses, has rights of survivorship (when one owner dies, the other automatically owns the entire property) and also requires joint action before property may be sold. Because neither may sell his or her share, both parties are protected. This is, in many states, the assumed form of ownership by wife and husband; if you want a different arrangement, it will have to be specified when you take title.

Joint tenancy also has a right of survivorship, but either owner can sell his or her interest and force a division of the property. It is the typical form of husband-wife ownership in states that do not recognize tenancy by the entirety.

Tenancy in common does not have survivorship rights and is more often used by business partners than by spouses. Yet Ann Seifert—remember the "Separate Property System" discussed earlier?—recommends that a married couple buy property, even a house, as tenants in common. If you do, she says in *His, Mine and Ours*, then you can specify the precise share of property you own. "If one partner dies, his share can be willed to the surviving spouse. In divorce, a settlement can be based on the value of each share of the property, because it had been clearly identified beforehand."

This approach may seem cold-blooded, but it may also make practical sense for some people. In any case, the Research Institute of America noted, "there is a clear trend today for prospective spouses to keep in individual name any property they own when they enter marriage. For the sake of simplifying any conflicts of interest that may occur later, many lawyers and financial advisors recommend, too, that property acquired during the marriage be put in one name or the other, on whatever basis seems most appropriate to your particular circumstances . . . . Such separate ownership can eliminate a host of potential personal and legal problems later on."

You probably *will* want to own your family home jointly, with rights of survivorship, because a home is as much an emotional symbol as a financial investment. It may be necessary to do so, in any case, if both incomes are required to support the purchase. But what about other property you may acquire? The more you acquire, the more complicated the ownership question becomes. There are income tax and estate tax implications, and you should be sure to consult a good tax attorney or accountant. At the outset, however, when you don't own much, some simple rules will suffice:

• Cars should probably be owned individually so that, in case of a lawsuit stemming from an accident, only the owner's assets are subject to collection.

• Investments should probably be made individually, as well, so that quick action to take advantage of a rising (or falling) stock market won't be stymied because one partner is on the road. To keep things "fair," you might take turns making investments that are roughly equivalent in dollar value (the *types* of investments may not be the same because one of you may prefer to be conservative, as discussed earlier, while the other enjoys taking a fling).

• Vacation homes, if located in another state, should definitely be owned jointly so that they pass directly to the survivor. Otherwise both states, the state of primary residence and the state where the vacation home is situated, may insist on probating the will and assessing inheritance tax.

• Safe deposit boxes to safeguard your valuables can be of the "his" and "hers" variety, with each of you renting an individual box and giving your spouse the right of access as your deputy. *His* individually owned property should be in *her* box, and vice versa. In most states a safe deposit box is sealed upon the death of the owner (or of a co-owner), with access restricted until tax authorities have reviewed the contents. Two separate boxes will let you get at your property in the event of your spouse's death.

The Fine Art of Negotiating

Traditionally, as we've seen, marital roles were clearcut. Women made decisions about home and children; men made decisions about economics and the outside world. If you didn't like the arrangement, you didn't get married. Today, the picture has changed, and, Bjorksten and Stewart report, "negotiating who does what is an expected part of the marital adjustment."

Those negotiations, as you've probably already realized, are at their peak in the early years of marriage. This, after all, is when you're finding out about each other...and about yourself. It's the time when you may realize that your wife has a habit of buying expensive gifts for friends and family, or that your husband thinks nothing of putting off paying bills until the past-due notice arrives. It's the time when you may find out that she is perfectly willing to take help from parents while you would rather stand on your own two feet, or that he says you're equal partners but would just as soon not hear about your promotion. It may even be a time when you decide that your partner is not quite rational about money...or simply that you can't stand what he or she is doing.

You have a lot of things to sort out when you're first married—attitudes toward parental help, toward your own paychecks, toward the way you spend and the way you make decisions. Rather than rely on internalized expectations, put your expectations on the table; talk them through. Rather than let emotions rule your behavior, which is likely to lead either to unending conflict or to the kind of money behavior that may undermine your marriage, learn to negotiate.

Let's assume that you've rejected the traditional version of marriage, in which the man unilaterally makes the financial decisions. You're going to make your decisions together. But there are several ways to make decisions, no one of which will work every time:

• Mutual agreement is ideal but, in this all too real world, it isn't always possible.

• Accommodation, in which you agree to disagree, may be appropriate in some situations; using individual accounts to make different types of investments, suiting your different temperaments, is a good example.

• Compromise means finding a middle ground:
Investing in mutual funds is too stodgy, in commodities
too risky, so you pool your money in good growth stocks.

• Concession, where one of you simply gives in to
the other, is least desirable but may happen from time
to time, especially if there is an issue one of you feels
strongly about and the other doesn't. There's nothing
wrong with concession, in fact, as long as it isn't always
the same partner making the concessions.

On issues where you aren't willing to go your separate
ways, don't want to make concessions, but still can't reach
a mutually agreeable solution, try brainstorming. In this
tried-and-true technique you put forth every possible
solution to a particular problem, not just the solution
you're each fixed on, in a quest for a new and original
answer that will suit you both. If you're brainstorming
about investment possibilities, for example, as I pointed
out in *The Lifetime Book of Money Management*, you
won't get locked into a battle over CDs versus GNMAs.
Instead, you'll run through every type of investment that
comes to mind, from a savings account to an oil-and-gas
exploration deal. An even-tempered verbal free-for-all—
don't interrupt each other, don't raise your voices, and
don't discard any suggestion as too preposterous—should
provide a wide-ranging menu of alternatives. Only when
the menu is complete, when neither of you can think of
another thing, should you consider the merits of each
investment possibility. Discard the ones that either of
you violently opposes; there should be enough remaining
items for consideration.

Assess the remaining alternatives in terms of how well
they meet your previously determined goals and objectives. Look at the consequences of each alternative: Is
there a reasonable chance of making a profit on the
investment? Will money have to be tied up for a long
time? What are the tax implications? What's the actual
degree of risk? You should ask yourself these questions
on any investment you might make individually as well.
With a joint investment decision, however, finish up with

one more question: Will you still be speaking to each
other if the investment doesn't pan out?

There's no reason to be upset if you discover after the
ceremony that you and your partner have different attitudes toward money—as long as you each take the trouble to understand the other's perspective and negotiate
your marital spending patterns. Understanding and
negotiation both rely on communication. In addition to
brainstorming about specific things like investment
opportunities or career options or where to live, take the
time to talk about fundamentals: Where would you each
like to be, financially, five years down the road? What
material things are important to you? What do you define
as a necessity and what as a luxury? How do you feel
about going into debt? How do you feel, really feel, about
keeping separate accounts? Do a little fantasizing too:
What would you do, right now, if you suddenly came
into $10,000?

If you do run into money conflicts, don't let them
fester. And don't let grievances accumulate until you spill
out three years of irritation in one afternoon of screaming.
"You're completely irresponsible...You *had* to buy that
Cuisinart, and you've never used it since." Good communication techniques will help you tackle the problem
that is actually at hand without alienating your partner.
It's important to know, writes Carol Tavris, Ph.D., author
of *Anger: The Misunderstood Emotion*, when to speak
(preferably not when you are feeling angry), how to speak
(attack the problem, not the partner), and how to listen
(without interruptions).

Money Traps in Marriage

To keep money problems to a minimum:
• Establish a budget so that neither of you has to
account for every penny, but set a dollar limit on what
each of you will spend without consulting the other

(otherwise you may set your own mental limits, but they may not mesh).

• Set up checking accounts and credit cards in each partner's name so that you don't have to ask each other for money, but do consult on major purchases so that you don't run up excessive debt.

• Review your financial affairs on a regular basis, and be sure you're both informed (not just whoever does the bookkeeping) about the state of your financial union.

• · Keep a step ahead by forecasting your financial life stages: What will you do when you get a raise? What will happen to your finances when you have a baby? What if you take time out for grad school?

• Try to be objective about money, to remove it as a source of conflict in your relationship. Acknowledge that behavior with money may reflect unconscious emotional needs, but don't play amateur psychologist and don't "diagnose" your spouse.

• Communicate. Don't assume that you know what your partner wants or how your partner will decide a given issue. Don't assume that your partner knows what you want if you keep the information to yourself.

· 5 ·

After Divorce: Alone Again

MARRIAGES DISSOLVE for many reasons—too many
arguments over money, disagreement over how to raise
children, competitiveness in jobs, one partner's growing
away from the other, simple incompatibility of the sort
that makes you wonder why you ever got married in the
first place. Whatever the underlying reason or the final
impetus, as sociologist John Gagnon wrote in *Working
Mother*, "When a marriage dissolves today, money is the
medium through which disappointments, fears and anger
are expressed." Money, in fact, "is the last residue of
the relationship itself." Money, and the things it buys,
becomes loaded with all the feelings of anger, bitterness,
and betrayal that can't be expressed in any other way.

Valerie and Jim, for example, both agreed that their
marriage was over. Both thought they could handle an
amicable divorce. Yet when it came down to dividing
the property they'd amassed over six years of marriage,
amicability disappeared. The wrangling reached fever
pitch over their collection of folk song records. Not that
the records were particularly valuable. But they did represent happier times, afternoons spent choosing records
and evenings spent listening.

The scenario continues after the marriage itself is dissolved. Sometimes it's arguments over maintenance payments (today's term for alimony) or child support.
Sometimes it's a matter of one "ex" buying something
the other always wanted and could not afford. "The min-

ute Jim moved out," Valerie says with some bitterness, "he bought himself the compact disk player I'd been wanting. He 'couldn't afford it' when we were married; now, all of a sudden, there's no problem." Since Jim made a point of seeing to it that she knows about the player, his motive is clearly revenge. He may also be saying, "You'll be sorry. Look what you could have had if we'd stayed together."

Marital money games—the way we act out dependency and exert power—can and frequently do continue after the divorce decree is final. They are particularly likely to continue when the ex-partners are linked by children. And they are exacerbated by the practical reality that financial standing suffers after divorce, just as a feeling of emotional abandonment takes hold.

Divorced men and women represented 9 percent of the ever-married population in 1984, compared with 4 percent in 1970 and just 3 percent in 1960. Yet, says the Census Bureau, the rate of divorce in the United States has leveled off. Maybe it had to. As Andrew Scherlin, a sociologist at Johns Hopkins University, put it to *The New York Times:* "The climbing divorce rate had to stop somewhere or we'd find ourselves with 110 percent of all married couples getting divorced." But the rate is still high, and 50 percent of all people getting married today will get divorced in the future. This may be due, at least partially, to the fact that more women can now afford to walk out of unsatisfactory marriages. There's no way of knowing for sure, but anecdotal evidence clearly indicates that many of our mothers remained in unhappy marriages because, without an independent income, they were stuck. The woman who had to get walking-around money from her husband was (and is) a dependent woman.

This thesis finds verification in an unexpected quarter: The federal government offered an experimental income maintenance program to poverty-level women in an effort, in Dr. Pepper Schwartz's words in *Vogue,* to "take some of the volatility out of their lives and make their marriages more secure. What happened instead was an enormous increase in the divorce rate. A lot of women got out of

miserable situations that they would have gotten out of
a lot sooner if they had had any choice whatsoever.
Whereupon, the government immediately stopped the
study."

The more money a woman earns the more likely it
may be that she will end up divorced. Census Bureau
data as early as 1978 show that women in the $25,000 to
$50,000 bracket were divorced at a rate more than twice
the average for all women. When women earned over
$50,000 a year, the divorce rate jumped to four times
the average. But the reasons aren't clear: Are high-earning women "married" to their jobs? Do men find high-
earning women too competitive and therefore less desirable? Or do women with high incomes divorce because
they can afford to maintain their own households? The
reasons undoubtedly are complex. But when a woman
earns an income of her own, whether as a file clerk or a
vice-president, she is no longer totally dependent. Once
she can stand on her own feet, financially, she can leave
a marriage that has become intolerable.

But having an income of one's own doesn't blunt the
financial realities of divorce. Whether she leaves him,
he walks out on her, or both agree to split, both men
and women suffer when two households must be supported on the amount of money that formerly supported
one. But women suffer more. An often cited California
study by Lenore J. Weitzman measured the living standard of a group of Los Angeles County residents one year
after their divorce. The men experienced a 42 percent
improvement in their standard of living; the women suffered a 73 percent drop in theirs. While household income
typically declines for both parties after a divorce, adjustments for household size (in other words, the woman
usually gets the children) reveal that the man has more
purchasing power after the divorce while the woman has
much less.

The financial problems of older women are typically
more severe. These are the women who most often fall
into the category of "displaced homemaker"—women
whose "job" in life was maintaining a household. It's a

worthwhile job, it can even be a dignified one, but the pay isn't very good. In fact, the pay is nonexistent. Household work may be "worth" $10,000 to $15,000 a year (the Department of Consumer Economics and Housing at Cornell University's College of Human Ecology does some intricate studies showing a wide range of housework values, depending on children's ages, etc.), but that work is not reflected in the gross national product, in Social Security payments for homemakers, in pension plans, or, all too often, in divorce settlements. If it is awarded a value by the divorce court, the chances of collecting are slim.

The homemaker, no matter how valuable her contribution to her family in general and to her husband's career in particular (typing reports, playing hostess, etc.), is dependent on a male breadwinner for support. When she is left on her own, through divorce or death, her work loses its value at the same time that she loses her income. Thus, older divorcées and widows are the new poor, in what has been aptly called the "feminization of poverty." In one study the National Organization for Women found that 40 percent of all divorced white women who did not remarry within seven years had incomes that fell below the poverty level at least once. Of these, fully 20 percent were continuously close to poverty. The older a woman is at divorce, the less likely she is to remarry and the more difficult it is to find a job. Forty years of homemaking do not equip women to be financially independent. Some younger women, mostly mothers, also become poor as a result of divorce. JoAnn was only 36 when her husband walked out, leaving her with five children aged 2 weeks to 15 years. He subsequently became president of his company. He also married a younger woman with a good income of her own. JoAnn does part-time word processing for a temporary agency and buys her children's clothes second-hand.

Younger displaced homemakers (when they are not held back by the demands of caring for small children) may become self-supporting, through job training, more readily than their older counterparts. When older women are divorced, even by their own choice, they frequently face serious and ongoing financial difficulty. But financial know-how can help. When a New Jersey woman was told by her husband of forty years that he wanted out, that she would have to sell the house and get a job, she was devastated, sure she'd be out on the streets. After a friend told her to ask about his pension, the picture changed. A trade-off was made. She relinquished rights to his pension; in exchange, she kept the house and received alimony.

The family home is often a couple's single largest asset. It's also the emotional focus of family life. Little wonder that wrangles over the house play a major role in divorce proceedings. She may want to stay in the house, claiming it wouldn't be fair to uproot the kids. He may want the proceeds of a sale to get on with his new life. But emotions can run just as high over much smaller items. "He may want the ashtray because he bargained the price down to $2.00," Linda Bird Francke wrote in *Growing Up Divorced*. "She may want it because it is the precise color of red she has always loved and rarely found." The ashtray itself is insignificant. But it can be the focus of a firestorm as one of "the spoils of marriage. After all, even a bad marriage is a part of one's history, and everybody wants the best of the artifacts."

The trade-offs are never easy. And, at any age, the emotional costs of divorce are staggering. Even when a divorce starts out to be amicable, as Valerie and Jim found out, legal and financial maneuvering can destroy whatever vestige of feeling the partners still had for each other. The maneuvering, both before and after the decree is final, can be an intense replay of all the money games of marriage.

Is Anyone at Fault?

As long as a man and a woman remain married, by and large they can arrange the ownership and control of their property any way they like. As soon as they decide to divorce, the law becomes a party to their decisions.

And the law, although it varies from state to state, has undergone a revolution in recent years. The revolution is twofold. First is the nationwide trend toward "no-fault" divorce, where both parties can simply agree that divorce is desired without assigning blame to either. Second is the principle of "equitable distribution."

No-fault was intended to be a step forward, away from the tacky days of private detectives amassing evidence of adultery. And, indeed, it's a lot more civilized. But it has had some not-so-wonderful consequences. First, in the opinion of many observers, it has made divorce too easy. (Without taking a moral stand on the issue, divorce is never easy.) Second, and perhaps more important in terms of this discussion, no-fault has drastically changed property settlements in divorce. If no one is at fault, even if someone has in fact walked out, then no one "deserves" to receive more or less of the couple's property.

"Equitable distribution" carries through on this notion. Once upon a time there were eight community property states (Arizona, California, Idaho, Louisiana, Nevada, New Mexico, Texas, and Washington) in which the presumption was that all property acquired during a marriage was jointly owned. The other forty-two states generally adhered to the principle of title: The person whose name was on the property owned the property, without regard to whose money went toward making the purchase. The wife whose income supported the family while the husband's income went toward investments, nominally for "their" future, was the wife who wound up with nothing after the divorce because all of "their" investments were in his name. And the wife who worked side by side with her husband for twenty or thirty years, whether on a farm or in a business, similarly owned nothing (not even Social Security benefits) if he had retained title.

There are still the same eight community property states, although their laws are not uniform. The rest of the states have moved away from title law toward the concept of equitable distribution, providing that marital property is divided at divorce according to both its source and the need of the parties without regard to title. (If you've moved from one state to another during your marriage and the states have different rules, you may find distribution of property at divorce a confusing mess. In some instances, acquisition of property must be traced back to a particular state and division of that property done according to the laws of that state. The Uniform Marital Property Act, when and if it is widely adopted, will help to end this confusion.)

Property, meanwhile, has been subject to an ever-broadening definition. In some jurisdictions it includes accrued pension benefits of a not-yet-retired spouse. It can include a share in a spouse's business. It can even include a share in yet-to-be-earned income from a profession. In a well-publicized New York case, Loretta O'Brien won a portion of her former husband's future earnings from the practice of medicine. The New York Court of Appeals, in its landmark decision, ruled that "marital property" is "all property acquired by either or both spouses during the marriage, regardless of the form in which it is held." Under this definition, Michael O'Brien's medical license was marital property, subject to equitable distribution.

But a split of marital property, whether that property is a house, a pension, or a medical license, is not automatic. It may be necessary to fight. Loretta O'Brien fought through three courts of law because, she claimed, her earnings had made Michael O'Brien's medical license possible. Other women (and men as well) have other grounds for complaint. "I worked for my husband for thirteen and a half years of marriage, without a salary, because the accountant said paying me would make my husband's tax bracket too high. Now he's left and I have nothing. But I'm not settling for nothing. I want a share of the business *and* I want alimony." This wife has reason to be angry, but she may or may not win her case. Whether or not she wins, the battle itself is sure to be costly. One estimate indicates that the average contested divorce costs each party $9,000; where there is substantial property (business interests, stocks and bonds, perhaps a vacation house) the costs are considerably higher. Legal fees have risen sharply under equitable distribution laws, with the need to ferret out property, get it appraised, and ascertain who owns what.

When a divorce does go to trial, in an equitable distribution state, the presiding judge may consider a number of factors: the length of the marriage, the contribution of each spouse to the accumulation of assets, the employability of each spouse, who has custody of children, and, yes, whose name is on the title. Joint ownership is no longer a controlling factor but, notes Harriet N. Cohen, president of the New York Women's Bar Association, it certainly is weighed by the courts in determining who is entitled to what. The judge decides, in each individual case, what equitable means. Where you divorce, therefore, still makes a difference—if you're rich enough to have a choice. John DeLorean and Christina Ferrare fought a well-publicized battle over whether their legal residence was in California (a 50-50 community property state, which she wanted) or New Jersey (an equitable distribution state, which he preferred). DeLorean won half the battle: He kept his fortune, in a New Jersey ruling, but lost custody of his children.

Equitable distribution may be fairer in concept than title, but it was never intended to mean equal distribution. There is no assurance of a 50-50 split. Even the value of the family home can be split 60-40, 70-30, or not at all; in a great many cases, where the home is a couple's largest asset, it must be sold under the terms of the agreement so that there are assets to share. It's slowly being realized, as a result, that women and children are coming out farther and farther behind. That's because equitable distribution, once hailed by women's groups as a boon for women, has combined with no-fault divorce in many instances to reduce financial support. In usually progressive New York State, as an example, it's been estimated that women and children get just 25 to 30 percent of the marital property.

In general, where once a woman could count on raising her children in the family home, that home is increasingly likely to be sold out from under her. With her share of the proceeds, in the face of high housing costs, she can seldom find an equivalent place to live. Where once a woman whose husband was at fault in a divorce could count on alimony, today "income maintenance" may be granted for a short-term period (typically two years) to enable that woman to get back on her feet financially. Where a woman has not held a paying job in many years, or where she must care for small children, short-term maintenance is simply not enough. Where a lump sum settlement takes the place of alimony, a woman who is unsophisticated in financial matters and is in emotional turmoil in the aftermath of divorce may spend unwisely. One such woman went through $70,000 in under a year.

And, although both no-fault divorce and equitable distribution were meant to minimize maneuvering, they haven't done so. It may no longer matter in a strictly legal sense whose name is on the ownership papers, but it's become vitally important to "prove" just what contribution each has made to the marriage. Did she scrimp and save to stretch his salary? Prove it. Did he moonlight at an extra job to put her through school? Prove it. Should she have a share in his accumulated pension? or his professional practice? Prove it. Was it money from his parents that provided the down payment on their house? Prove it. The need for record-keeping, it seems, is greater than ever.

Savvy partners win out over naive partners every time. "I filed for divorce two months before receiving the balance of my grandmother's estate," says one man. "If I'd waited till I turned thirty, when I got the money, it would have gone into the pot and my wife would have shared it." An older woman, once widowed and once divorced, kept the proceeds of an accident settlement in her own name during her second marriage, even though her husband—they were still married at the time—"ranted and raved. I wouldn't give in," she says now; "I don't know if I had a premonition, but I knew I needed that money for my own security."

Divorce mediation is an attempt to avoid the legal maneuvering, the high costs, and the emotional residue of contested divorce. With a mediator acting as a referee, the theory goes, a couple can work out its own divorce settlement. But not everyone thinks mediation is a good idea, especially where sizable assets exist. The less sophisticated spouse, without expert assistance to dig into financial records, may lose out. As one lawyer puts it, mediation often means "selling someone down the river, generally the woman."

The situation is rough for both parties to a divorce. Where a couple was affluent, the burden of supporting two households may leave both barely middle-class. Where there are few assets to begin with, everyone can wind up poor. The financial realities are harsh. So is the emotional fallout.

No matter what the lawyers do, no matter what the judges do, neither partner ever feels that a divorce settlement is "fair." Maybe it can't be. Where there are significant assets, one partner (most often, again, the man because he *has* more assets) may try to hide them from the other. Some men have been known to deliberately leave phony income tax returns around the house. Others establish their own bank accounts, conceal business profits, and overstate losses—all relatively easy to do with a spouse who doesn't pay attention to financial matters. Many men, Lenore J. Weitzman writes in *The Divorce Revolution*, manage to delay salary increases and bonuses until after the divorce is final, thus reducing assets subject to court award. Many businesses and professional practices suddenly go downhill in the year before divorce becomes final, only to pick up again afterward. Some even change ownership. "My husband took over a busi-

ness from his father when his father retired. I was led
to believe that he owned half and his mother owned half.
Now I find that his mother owns the whole thing. I
trusted him, and all our money went into the business
that his mother owns. I don't even have a bank account."

If *you* sense that a divorce may be in the wings, and
you're the partner with fewer assets:

• Do open your own bank account and secure your
own individual credit. You needn't go as far as the woman
who squirreled away $20,000 from the grocery money
over twenty years of marriage, but you should have some
funds in your own name. If you stay happily married
you'll be able to use the money to buy your spouse a
gift, or provide you both with security in an emergency.
If you don't, it might provide survival.

• Write to the Internal Revenue Service for copies
of your last few tax returns, if you don't have them; your
spouse doesn't have to sign the request and you can have
the forms sent to you at your office or in care of a friend.

• Start to pay attention to household finance and to
keep track of household expenditures. Knowing how much
it actually costs to run your household and being able to
document the information can carry a lot of weight during
a court hearing.

• Check on the balance in joint bank accounts (call
or visit the bank) and on securities holdings (call the
stockbroker). Make a record, preferably in snapshots or
video, of any antiques or art that you both have collected
over the years.

• Don't overlook "hidden" assets such as life insurance policies or your spouse's pension. Becoming an
irrevocable beneficiary of life insurance on your spouse,
paid for by your spouse, is a good way to ensure ongoing
support. A pension may also be an important asset; it
may even be worth more than the mortgaged family
home when its future annual value is expressed in today's
dollars in a lump sum. In most states, pensions are now
considered marital property and are subject to division

by court order. Whether you go after the insurance or the pension or both, both are bargaining chips in divorce negotiations.

• Become informed. Take a course in money management, read books and magazines, send away for the brochures offered by financial institutions. You owe it to yourself—and to your children, if you have any— to put yourself in control.

Tax Rules of the Road

You and your about-to-be-former spouse may actually agree on property divison, continuing support, and the rest. But don't formalize your agreement until you include Uncle Sam in your calculations. Tax laws can make a big difference in who comes out ahead and by how much. Major changes in the tax code in 1984 simplified matters somewhat, but don't sit back and relax. New rules on property settlements, alimony payments, and exemptions for dependent children will have a major impact on how you accommodate the economics of divorce.

The new rule on *property settlements*, which affects all property transfers made after July 18, 1984, marks a major change. Suppose husband and wife own the family home jointly. When that home became the sole property of one partner, under the old law, the transfer was considered a sale. If the home had appreciated in value, as most homes do, the "selling" partner could owe a hefty capital gains tax on any profit over and above the value of the original half-ownership. He might have had difficulty paying that tax, because the property was not really sold and no cash found its way into his pocket, but the IRS is unconcerned with such trivialities.

The same tax rules applied when any property was transferred, whether that property was individually or jointly owned and whether it was a car or securities or whatever; the partner making the transfer of a half or whole interest (even if on court order) could be hit with a sizable tax bill. The receiving partner could then turn around and sell the property without paying tax on the gain. This law, according to the New Jersey Society of Certified Public Accountants, "resulted in financial acrobatics so that a divorce settlement could be structured to avoid paying tax on the gain." This is no longer the case.

Under the new law, there is no gain or loss to either party at the time of the settlement. The transfer is considered a gift. Should the recipient then sell the property, however, tax will be due. Some observers believe that this is as big a burden on the recipient (typically the wife) as the previous law was on the transferer (typically the husband). But one good thing can be said about the change: No tax will be due until the property is sold, and the sale itself should result in enough cash to make the payment. In any case, if you are the recipient, be sure to keep careful records. Your expenditures for closing costs, home improvements, and so on can reduce any capital gains tax that is due at a later date.

You might also think carefully, if you have a choice, about just which assets you accept. Barbara found herself faced with a choice between two assets, each worth $100,000: the family's vacation house, or jointly owned securities. The house consumed money in maintenance; the securities provided dividend income. The house could be used and enjoyed; the securities represented cold cash. But there's another issue. Barbara's attorney pointed to the tax consequences of her choice. The house was originally purchased for $45,000, the stock for $20,000. If she later sells the asset she accepts now, for any reason, she will owe a lot more capital gains tax on the profit in the securities. If she really has a choice, and if she doesn't need the current income, she should take the house. But most women, in need of support, should take the asset most readily convertible to cash. An equal distribution of assets, in fact, may not mean as much as liquidity.

Dependency exemptions have also been clarified. Under the old law, the parent who provided the most money for the support of the child was granted the income tax dependency exemption. But it could be very difficult to prove who provided the bulk of the support and the child could become a victim in another tug of war between the parents. "He lived with me, and I had all the day in-day out expenses as well as all the responsibility," as one mother puts it. "But his father claimed the exemption. He said the orthodonture bills pushed his contributions over half. I don't believe it." Under the new rule, this mother gets both the responsibility and the exemption. The parent who has custody of the child for the greater portion of the year is entitled to claim the exemption unless that right to the exemption is waived in writing. The person making the claim can change from year to year, depending on who stands to gain the most. What's more, the exemption is no longer an all-or-nothing proposition. You can give up the dependency exemption and still claim the child's medical expenses. In fact, you may both claim medical expenses as long as you both meet the basic rule that medical expenditures, as a whole, exceed a set percent of your gross income. If only one of you is in that position, one of you should claim the deduction. Or the higher-income parent might consider allowing the lower-income parent to claim these deductions, because they're then worth more. That's assuming you and your former spouse can discuss such matters.

Alimony is still, under the new law, deductible by the paying spouse and taxable to the recipient. But the new law makes both property settlements and child support (neither of which is deductible) harder to disguise as alimony in order to claim a deduction. Effective with divorce decrees issued after December 31, 1984, annual alimony payments in excess of $10,000 must now be continual for at least six years in order to be deductible. Alimony cannot be pegged to any event in a child's life; it can't stop, for example, when a child turns eighteen, goes off to college or gets married. And there are stiff tax penalties if alimony payments in any year decrease by more than $10,000 below payments in any preceding year. Divorcing spouses may still vengefully seek to manipulate alimony payments, but both should try instead to take maximum advantage of the tax laws. Try to look at your arrangement as a business deal, so that you both can retain your dignity. And get competent tax advice; in the light of the new rules, it's more important than ever.

One positive note: Alimony may now be counted as income for the purpose of opening an Individual Retirement Account. This means that both spouses can claim a tax deduction: the giver of alimony because alimony, in full, is deductible, and the recipient for the amount, up to $2,000, contributed to an IRA.

The *child care credit*, permitting the custodial parent to claim the costs of child care incurred so that the parent could work, was previously available only to the custodial parent who also claimed the dependency exemption. Now this credit, which can be worth up to $720 for one child or $1,440 for two or more children (depending on your income; see p. 151 for details), may be claimed by the custodial parent whether or not he or she qualifies for the dependency exemption. Expenses that qualify for the credit include babysitters, housekeepers, day care centers, and, usually, summer camp. Paying Aunt Nell will also qualify, as long as Aunt Nell is not your dependent.

The Single Parent

Divorce is seldom simple. When there are dependent children, however, the financial and emotional complications are often immense. Questions of custody and of child support must be resolved. Then, unless parents remarry, life must go on as a single-parent household.

Custody

When Arthur and Rosalie agreed on a divorce, their daughter Alison was only 3 years old. Rosalie assumed that she would get custody of her small daughter. But Arthur decided that he wanted custody. He got it, too, based on his plans to remarry and a judge's assumption that a two-parent household would provide a better home for Alison than a one-parent household in which her mother had to work.

This judge's decision would have been remarkable just a few years ago, when children of "tender years" almost invariably were given over into the custody of their mothers. No longer. Changing divorce laws have had a marked impact on child custody as well. Now that "no-fault" is the game and "equitable distribution" the rule by which the game is played, both mothers and fathers, in many jurisdictions, have an equal chance at custody.

It's terrific that today's fathers care enough about their small children to want to raise them. But some professionals are concerned. One problem is that bitter court battles over custody can't help but affect the children. Another is that, in some cases, children become the bargaining chip in a game for high economic stakes. Sometimes the family home is at stake as a custody battle rages, because parents assume (not always accurately) that the one who gets custody will also get to keep the house. Sometimes child support is at issue. Richard Neely, a justice on the West Virginia Supreme Court of Appeals and author of *The Divorce Decision*, points to the "sinister bargaining" that goes on when men offer to relinquish custody in exchange for lower child support. The wife who wins this battle may lose the war in the end, because accepting lower child support may mean raising the child in poverty. When men really want custody they often manage to get it, both because their higher incomes can make it possible to wage a protracted legal battle and because some judges (and some mothers too) are convinced that a higher income can better support a child. It doesn't help if a mother would be forced to sell the family home in order to raise money to supplement low wages.

Either way, according to a 1985 report by the New

York State Law Revision Commission, the relationship
between the child and the noncustodial parent often suffers in the wake of a legal battle over custody. The reason:
The losing parent, believing the child has been lost forever, may withdraw financial and emotional support. The
commission has proposed that court-assigned mediators
help parents work out mutually acceptable custody
arrangements if they cannot do so on their own.

Custody, of course, isn't always a battle. Some parents
agree that one or the other is the best to raise the children. And some agree on joint custody. If you agree on
single-parent custody, you probably also agree that the
noncustodial parent will keep in touch. How much you
do "keep in touch" depends in part on just how bitter
you are after the divorce. Relatively few divorced parents
are able to put on a "family" front for the children, but
you should try to discuss their needs objectively with
your former spouse and be present emotionally for the
children. Within a couple of years, unfortunately, many
noncustodial parents drop out of their children's lives.
The reason: Sporadic contact is just too painful for everyone concerned. The result: alienation from your children, and their increasing financial need.

If you agree on joint custody, be sure you understand
that there are two different kinds. The Samsons employ
one variety; with joint legal custody, their three sons live
with their mother and periodically visit their father, but
both parents participate in decisions about education,
medical care, and the like. The Jordans do it differently.
They have joint physical as well as legal custody, and
their children, in the particular setup they've devised,
spend alternate weeks in each parent's home. This works
because the parents live near each other, so that school
and neighborhood playmates are the same, and because
the Jordans are able to cooperate for their children's
welfare.

Joint physical custody has received considerable attention in recent years. It can work well, for some children
and for some parents under some circumstances. But

some judges have awarded joint physical custody, even where the parents agreed that one of them should have sole custody, because they truly believe that joint custody is better for the children. Others award joint custody, some observers suspect, because it's easier than making a tough decision. If joint physical custody isn't truly desired by both parents, a judicial decision isn't going to make it work.

When everyone agrees on joint physical custody, it can have distinct advantages. It can benefit the children because they feel loved and wanted by both parents. It benefits parents who want to remain very much a part of their children's lives. But there are also potential disadvantages. Some children can't cope with moving from place to place. They become confused and anxious, partly because they must live in two different places and according to two sets of rules. They move between two homes, says Dr. Nancy Chiswick, adjunct professor of psychology at The Pennsylvania State University, "designed both in terms of the environment and in terms of the emotional climate by two different people, who are different enough that they couldn't get along in a marriage." Some parents, not surprisingly since they did divorce, find it impossible to communicate about the children or to cooperate in their behalf. And some parents start out able to handle joint custody, until one of them remarries or one moves to a distant location. Then, if the children are still dependent, the custody issue must be resolved once again.

Child Support

Interwoven with the custody issue, yet a separate issue of its own, child support has received a lot of attention in recent years. A bargaining chip in the custody battle, child support is a law honored far more in the breach than in the observance. When child support is actually paid, according to one study, it covers less than half the costs of child-rearing; the average award for two children is a scant $200 a month. And even this meager amount often isn't paid. A 1981 Census Bureau study showed that fewer than 60 percent of fathers are ordered to pay child support, and fewer than half of these actually make full payments. Of these, many stop paying by the time a year is up. Too many husbands simply ignore court judgments. Perhaps they are "punishing" their ex-wives. Whatever the reason, "It is well known," social psychologist Elizabeth Cauhapé writes in *Fresh Starts: Men & Women After Divorce*, that "immediately following many California divorces ex-husbands get their companies to transfer them out of state and, effectively, out of their obligations to children from a first marriage." California fathers are not alone.

But men are not villains. Men don't usually embark on divorce determined to rid themselves of children as well as wife. One of the problems may be that support payments must go to the ex-wife, who then spends the money on behalf of the children. Those children sometimes get funny ideas about the payments. "If my Daddy sends the money for me," asks a 9-year-old, "how come I don't get it to spend? How come Mommy says there's no money for ice skates, and then she buys a pocketbook?" Older children sometimes become downright manipulative, twisting guilt strings in both parents. It helps, as far as the children are concerned, to be as open as possible about the financial situation. And it helps, with the noncustodial parent, to involve him in the children's lives. "Men who are allowed to take an active part in the decisions that affect their children, perhaps even to have some input about how the support money is spent," says social scientist Paul Bohannan in *All the Happy Families*, "have far better records of making their support payments."

Sometimes, too, separation of father and children is nobody's fault. A mother remarries and moves hundreds or thousands of miles away. Her ex-husband can't afford to visit, or to pay the children's way to him, and gradually he loses touch. As he becomes increasingly distant from his children's lives, he has less motivation to send money. Then, if he remarries and starts a new family, he may have no motivation at all.

Lower-income fathers have a better record than middle-income fathers when it comes to financial support, according to a recent study by researchers at the Bush Institute for Child and Family Policy at the University of North Carolina at Chapel Hill. Lower-income fathers also seem to remain closer to their children. They are more likely to remain in the same neighborhood and to take an active role in their children's daily lives. Middle-class fathers are more likely to lose contact with their children after divorce has broken contact with the mother. They are particularly likely to lose contact with the children of a first marriage if they remarry and start new families. In a poignant memoir of his own "lost" family, novelist C. W. Smith wrote in *Esquire,* "Years ago I called a college buddy I hadn't heard from in a while. He had divorced his first wife but had remarried. I asked him how many kids he had now. 'Just the one.' 'One? I thought you had two.' '*Aw* hell!' he snorted. 'You're thinking of the ones I had with Judy. They don't count.'"

Once again, everybody suffers. Resentful fathers charge that mothers deny visitation rights in an effort to squeeze more money. Bitter mothers point to the affluent lifestyles of their ex-husbands and wonder why they can't support their own children. And what you wind up with, Nancy Chiswick of Penn State points out, is "not only the withdrawal of the emotional support and love but the withdrawal of the financial support. . . . It makes a tremendous impact on [a] child's life to grow up in poverty and yet probably typically with middle class values."

It isn't always a question of poverty. Elaine is the only child of a New York couple; her father is a lawyer, her mother an editor. Elaine grew up in a comfortable, book-lined apartment, attended private school, and, until recently, expected to attend a good private college. Now the lawyer and the editor have gone their separate ways. Elaine lives with her mother, who says, "On an editor's salary, I can't possibly send Elaine to any of the schools she always thought she'd attend. But how can I tell her I can't do it? How can I tell her to change all her hopes and dreams?" There's no hunger here—an editor's income buys ample food even if it won't pay for Harvard—but it's nonetheless hard on a child to switch the rules in the middle of the game. It's hard on a child when saved-up college tuition goes to pay divorce lawyers' fees. And it's hard on children to realize that, with the legal age of majority now 18 in most states, divorce settlements do not necessarily include any provision for college.

For many mothers and their children, college is far from the primary issue. Postdivorce existence is, if not hunger, a grinding kind of life. "I got the house and the kids," an Ohio woman says, "but he paid the child support maybe three or four times, then stopped. I sold my jewelry, I put off paying utility and tax bills, and I finally had to sell the house and move in with my mother."

With millions of dollars in unpaid child support and a growing awareness of the feminization of poverty, steps are being taken to enforce court decisions about child support. Until recently only welfare families could expect much help in collecting delinquent child support; only welfare mothers had access to absent fathers' salaries, property, and tax refunds. Effective in October 1985, however, federal legislation helps families of all kinds collect child support even if the delinquent parent has moved to another state. The new legislation enables states to place liens on personal property such as real estate and to withhold child support that is more than thirty days overdue from a parent's paycheck. Federal and state income tax refund checks may also be intercepted. Even unemployment compensation may be tapped when child support payments are delinquent. But states differ in their implementation of the child support enforcement program; check your local child support enforcement office (the number should be listed under your state or county social service agencies) for details.

The 1984 Child Support Enforcement Amendment is

a major step in the right direction. But, many observers
believe, it doesn't go far enough. Even if child support
payments are enforced, the payments may still be inadequate. Many fathers (it's still usually fathers who are
ordered to pay child support to custodial wives) can afford
to pay more. The 1985 Bush Institute study, sponsored
by the Social Security Administration and the Federal
Office of Child Support Enforcement, proposed a national
payment formula, based on a percentage of income, that
would allow children to share in the father's economic
status. For instance, *The New York Times* reported, while
a 1983 Bureau of the Census survey showed that the
average father was paying $2,460 a year in child support,
an experimental statewide formula in Delaware set the
average payment at $5,072. Almost identical results were
achieved with a similar percentage-of-income formula
established in Wisconsin in 1984 requiring the payment
of 17 percent of gross income for one child, 25 percent
for two, 29 percent for three, and 31 percent for four or
more. Under this Wisconsin formula the average male
wage-earner, earning $24,120 in 1984, would pay $6,281
toward the support of two children. This is more than
twice the current average payment. While a national
payment formula would be very helpful, if adopted, it
may not be enough. There is just too strong a prevailing
attitude that court-ordered child support can be ignored
at will. As a result, it's been suggested that child support
payments should be automatically deducted from paychecks without waiting for delinquency.

The solutions may be drastic. But, then, so are the
problems. And, when fathers and mothers use custody
and child support and visitation privileges as weapons,
it's the children who suffer. The money games are endless. Support checks are late. They bounce. They're
delivered via the children. "It makes me crazy," a mother
says, "when he hands the check, unfolded, to our thir-
teen-year-old. It makes me angry, it affects my relationship with my son, and there's nothing I can do to take
the smirk off my husband's face. I hate the money. I'm

humiliated that I'm dependent on this man's money coming in twice a month. But my children need it."

Many parents, saddened by having to tell children that they must do without, nonetheless agree (sometimes only in retrospect) that it can help build character. It doesn't hurt children to work or to weigh priorities in spending. But what does hurt is when children become victims of manipulation. One not-quite-18-year-old got a $14,000 pickup truck because his father cosigned a loan. Now the youngster must meet payments of $400 a month, money he must earn by working for his father. In another case, a teenage girl convinced her father that a high school band jacket would be a good buy; it would take the place of another coat and she could wear it through three years of high school. He agreed to share the cost. "Then," says her mother, "he said, 'Tell Mommy to put it on her charge card and I'll pay her when I can.' Now it's my problem. There's one hundred fifty dollars on my charge, and it's degrading for me to ask him for his share. The children see what he's doing." As an about-to-be-divorced person sums up, "Divorce is only about money. It's not about love or betrayal. It's about money, used as power, used as a stick to beat people with."

Raising Children Alone

Raising children after divorce, even when custody is shared, is significantly different from raising them before. It's hard on the children, either doing without one parent or splitting time between two households. And it's hard on the parents, on the custodial parent who must bear virtually full responsibility and on the noncustodial parent who may effectively lose contact with the children. With shared custody, as Penn State's Nancy Chiswick points out, parents must live two lives—one when they have the children and one when they are single. Not everyone can easily slip back and forth from one life style to another.

Single parents head 25.7 percent of all families, according to a 1985 Census Bureau report; that's up from 21.5 percent in 1980 and 12.9 percent in 1970. Of the 25.7 percent of single-parent households, 22.9 percent are headed by single mothers and 2.8 percent by single fathers. The children of divorce are no longer rarities, standing out from their peers. Many adjust well, especially if the predivorce household was full of acrimony. But that doesn't mean that the adjustment is easy, that the fallout from divorce misses them entirely. On the contrary. Young children may think the divorce is their fault. Older children are agonized, forced into parental roles by newly dependent parents. "In divorce," Lee Goldberg wrote in *Newsweek on Campus* in 1983, "parents seem to become teen-agers, and the kids become the adults. . . . Divorce didn't just split up our parents. It stole our childhood." Children of all ages may become manipulative, playing one parent against the other in seeking affection.

Parents agonize too. In single-parent families headed by mothers, the financial pressures are often intense. As Elaine's mother can no longer afford an Ivy League college, other mothers can't manage the music lessons or tennis rackets or name-brand sneakers that denote suburban acceptance. Some hold onto the family home by accepting help from relatives and by going into debt, so that the children can remain in familiar surroundings, but see those homes gradually deteriorate because there's no money for paint jobs, lawn care, or routine maintenance. Some must pull up stakes and move back into their own parents' home where they are treated, once again, as children. "My parents insisted that I stay home with my children. They wouldn't permit me to work. Permit!"

Single fathers, when they have custody, must cope with daily child care tasks they've never faced before and, when children are small, must often hire household help. When they don't have custody they frequently must take on two jobs in order to support two households. Financial conflicts, not surprisingly, frequently persist after divorce. It doesn't help if the need for extra

money is expressed with a psychological twist of the
knife, as in "Jennie should have a better music teacher,"
meaning, "If you really love your daughter, you'll come
up with the money." Both mothers and fathers also suffer
emotional trauma; psychologist Mavis Heatherington
notes, "We didn't find a single victimless divorce among
the families we studied." Most people eventually do cope,
but the period of adjustment is painful. There may be
less stress and conflict in the long run when an unhappy
marriage is dissolved, but the short run isn't easy. And
children inevitably suffer the consequences.

One study showed that divorced mothers often tried
to control children by being strict. Divorced noncustodial fathers, on the other hand, wanting limited time
spent with children to be as happy as possible, were
often excessively permissive and indulgent with the children. Many jump on a merry-go-round of activity during
visits, in what's been called the "Disneyland syndrome."
Others turn to material things. "Some of us pop irreg-
ularly into our children's lives, bearing an irrelevant or
even inappropriate gift," writes C. W. Smith, who bought
his son first a model airplane with a gasoline engine and
then a BB gun. The children, as a result, often become
cynical. "Mommy says Daddy doesn't give her any money,"
one 11-year-old reports, "but when we went to South
Street Seaport, he bought me a forty-two dollar koala
bear. Mommy wanted to know how he paid for it, and
I told her he charged it. I guess he's trying to make me
feel good because he doen't live here any more."

Custody is financially and socially hard on men as well
as women. "Dating is very expensive," says Edy Golish,
who runs a New Jersey support group called the Divorce
Experience, "and men in my group still like to treat
women like women. They get angry if a woman suggests
picking up the check. Many men even pay for babysitters
for their dates. And more men should realize that women
are often strapped financially, that they can't go out if
they can't afford a sitter." But sometimes the men themselves are strapped, which makes it very difficult to break

the lingering financial/emotional bonds of marriage. (Remarriage presents problems of its own, to be addressed in Chapter 6.)

Money Traps When You're Alone Again

• A head-in-the-sand approach to life, at any time, is dangerous. During divorce it can be ruinous. You owe it to yourself to know the financial facts of life and to be prepared to act on your own.

• Trading off rights during settlement negotiations, without fully understanding what you're doing, is a major mistake. Get competent legal advice, and be sure to consider:

Who will pay what toward the education of minor children (remember, legal responsibilities of parents now often end when children reach 18);

Provisions for health insurance for yourself and children (pending federal legislation may make ongoing coverage for dependents mandatory under on-the-job group contracts; meanwhile, continuation riders are sometimes available through group insurance, but you have to ask);

Pension rights and other employee benefits (they don't necessarily end at divorce).

• Marital money games, destructive for all concerned, can continue well beyond divorce. Try not to let this happen. Try to treat money objectively, and get on with your life.

· 6 ·

Marriage: The Second Time Around

IF YOU'RE getting married for the second time, you're likely to find it both a familiar experience and a strange one. Many of the issues are the same—developing a marriage style of your own, deciding how to handle your finances, resolving differing temperaments and attitudes—but the framework for the issues is new. You, and perhaps your spouse as well, are older, you may be better-fixed financially (if divorce hasn't taken its toll), and you're also the survivor(s) of previous marital experience. If *you* are not a survivor (frequently a never-married woman joins forces with a previously married man; sometimes the situation is reversed), you still must cope with the feelings generated in your spouse's prior marriage.

This is true whether the previous marriage ended by death or by divorce, but it's often more complicated with divorce. People who have been widowed may idealize the previous partner, thereby making it difficult to adapt to the new partner's way of doing things. But there's seldom the residue of bitterness that characterizes divorce, compounded by the financial constraints of dealing with property settlements, child support, and alimony.

Whether you're widowed or divorced, as you embark on a new marriage, do some money planning in advance. Plunging spontaneously into a first marriage, when assets and encumbrances are few, may be passed off as romantic love. Plunging headlong into a second marriage, especially when there are children, is nothing short of foolhardy.

When there are children—"his," "hers," and, sometimes, "theirs"—things get even more complicated and money problems, left unchecked, can poison the new relationship. Sometimes the problem is a court's doing. In reaction to the decision giving Loretta O'Brien a portion of the future income derived from her former husband's medical license, the Association of Divorced Fathers notes that the major victims are Dr. O'Brien's second wife and their two children.

But such court decisions, to date, are rare. More often the problem stems from an understandable eagerness to be out of the first marriage. "Geoff was so glad to have his freedom that he gave her everything," says a second wife about her predecessor. "He literally gave her everything but the clothes on his back, and *then* she got alimony too. We moved into a tiny studio apartment and lived on my income while everything he earned went to that bitch. I put up with it willingly at first, because I love Geoff, until I realized what it meant: I'll have to work until the day I die, I can never have a child of my own, we'll never have a decent place to live. It just isn't fair."

Geoff's first wife may indeed be on easy street, as his second wife surmises, but most divorcées with custody of children are closer to the poverty line. Reread Chapter 5 and you'll see what a difference one's perspective makes. But whether Wife No. 1 is rich or poor, Wife No. 2 suffers as well. So does the husband caught in the middle. And so, inevitably, do the children. When there isn't enough money to go around, and sometimes even when there is, money is the symbolic repository for emotions of all kinds.

And today's emotional battleground is extensive, as the players group and regroup in ever widening circles. Columnist Ellen Goodman describes a child patiently explaining a common situation to an adult for whom it wasn't common at all: "She had a friend who lived during the week with her mother and stepfather and half-brother. On some weekends, the stepfather's son visited with them, too, although he really lived with his mother and stepfather. On weekends, this friend went to visit with her father and stepmother, and the two children by her stepmother's first marriage. Of course, sometimes the stepbrothers weren't there because they were visiting their father and his wife and their children."

An adult view of this menage might go like this: The friend's stepfather supports her, his own son by her mother, and his son by his previous marriage. Her own father, who supports his stepchildren (when they aren't visiting their father), also contributes to her support. No one person may have ultimate responsibility. But everyone pays.

Merging Two Families

You may well find yourself, given today's divorce rate, in what's called a "blended" family. Whether that family contains three parts (because either you or your partner have been married before) or four (because you both have ties to previous families), you'll have some adjustments to make. Indeed, "three parts" and "four parts" may be a misstatement. Paul Bohannan, dean of the Division of Social Sciences and Communications at the University of Southern California, describes a much more complex family structure. In a simple four-member nuclear family, he says in *All the Happy Families*, there are a maximum of eight roles: a man who is both father and husband, a woman who is both mother and wife, youngsters who are both children and siblings. There are also eight possible relationships: husband-wife, father-son, and so on. A single-parent family has a correspondingly fewer number of relationships. But a blended or reconstituted family has an almost infinite number of relationships.

A family that is reconstituted by remarriage after the death of a partner, Bohannan says, is a simple stepfamily. It's not simple in the number of relationships—four step-parent relationships, three half-sibling relationships and three stepsibling relationships add up to as many as eighteen possible twosomes—but it isn't complicated "by the demands or the images of surviving natural parents outside the household."

Stepfamilies coming into being after divorce, however, "are more complex in their structure and *far* more complex emotionally." Now the relationships, especially as far as the children are concerned, expand in concentric circles involving parents and stepparents, siblings and stepsiblings and half-siblings. These assorted roles make the blended family almost a miracle of social complexity. It also makes it a psychological mine field.

Let's look at some possible situations, in order of complexity:

Situation 1: There are just two of you, you and your spouse, one of whom has been married before. There are no children. Your biggest problem, as with any newlyweds, may be deciding whether or not to pool your funds. In your case, however, the decision is complicated by one partner's prior experience of marriage. "I don't know whether Ken doesn't trust me, or whether he was just badly burned by his first wife's extravagance, but he absolutely refuses to open a joint account or have any joint investments. It's as if he has no faith in our marriage lasting." A divorced partner may indeed have little faith, at the outset, and may feel an urgent need for the security of separate funds. But faith can grow. It takes patience, and a willingness to live with separate accounts for the time being. After a while, you'll either find that separate accounts are working perfectly well and there's no reason to change, or separate bookkeeping will become a nuisance and you'll gradually merge your financial affairs as well as your lives.

Either way, it's important to be able to talk about what's bothering you, whether the issue is money or anything else. Sometimes an age gap between husband and wife, not uncommon in a second marriage, can trigger money problems. If he's in his fifties and comes into some money, he may want to invest it toward retirement; if she's in her thirties or early forties, with retirement a distant thought, she may dream of travel. Talking it through can produce a compromise.

Sometimes, even when ages are similar, the experience of a first marriage can make it difficult to bring up a particular subject in a second marriage. That subject may well be money. "Sam and I squabbled all the time about money, till it got to the point where I couldn't mention what something cost without him blowing up. Now I can't talk to Larry about money at all." Chances are, as marriage therapist Dr. Laura Singer puts it in describing a similar situation in *Stages: The Crises That Shape Your Marriage*, that "the ostensible subject— money—wasn't the real problem; rather it reflected other underlying difficulties between the partners, perhaps unresolved dependency needs or low self-esteem. Avoiding the subject in this marriage can only lead to trouble." It's natural to try to avoid the problems that undermined your first marriage, in other words, but it's also vital to remember that this is a new marriage, with new partners, new needs, and undoubtedly, new problems.

Some of these new problems will stem from your own individual expectations. Others will arise directly out of the previous relationship. Ken, for example, was waiting for his share of some property co-owned with his first wife. The property was to be sold, according to the terms of the divorce agreement, and the proceeds divided. Yet Wife No. 1 kept blocking the sale; although she needed money herself, it was more important to her to stand in Ken's way. Little wonder that Ken didn't want to own anything jointly with Wife No. 2!

If it were a first marriage for Ken and a second for his wife, there might be other problems. Women who have learned to be independent after death or divorce, whether they ever wanted to be independent or not, may expect to remain independent in a second marriage; a husband like Ken may or may not find that independence easy to take. When a woman (like a man) feels ripped off by the events that ended her first marriage, she may be particularly eager to hold on to some resources, "just in case." If she doesn't do so, if she turns everything over to the new husband in a display of trust and commitment, she may later have regrets.

That's what happened to one woman who had precariously structured financial independence in the five years between her marriages, then gave it up at her new husband's urging. "He needed the money from my house to wipe out some debts. I wanted us to start out fresh and clean so I gave him the money. Now I have no reserves at all and sometimes I'm scared. What will I do if this marriage doesn't work?"

Situation 2: One of you has children from a previous marriage but does not have custody. So you're still a two-person household, accept for the one weekend a month and school vacations when the children visit. The primary issue here, if the noncustodial spouse takes his responsibilities seriously, may be lack of money. Even if there are adequate funds, resentment can build up when a spouse diverts energies to supporting (and thinking about) a first family. When there really isn't enough money—when a second wife must continue to work or must put off having children—resentments can fester. As for the previously married spouse, he's caught in the middle. "I don't want anything to do with my first wife, but it means a lot to me to keep close to my children. Annie knew that when she married me."

But Annie *didn't* know that her own income would be counted in setting new child support levels for her husband's children. In many states courts look at total family income in making judgments; that income may well include money earned by a second spouse. Approximately one-third of a husband's and second wife's combined income, according to some estimates, is awarded to the husband's first wife and family. (That first wife may still have nowhere enough income to support herself and her children, as we've noted, but that doesn't make a second wife—who may want children of her own—feel any better. This is a classic no-win situation.)

Annie has another cause for resentment: As part of the divorce settlement, Art agreed to make his first wife the irrevocable beneficiary of his life insurance policy. The proceeds of that policy, when he dies, will replace (at least in part) the alimony and child support he currently pays, an arrangement Art accepted in the interests of his children. But what about Annie? With money short, there's no way to buy another life insurance policy. Will she be left to her own devices at Art's death?

Will she also be left childless, because of Art's financial obligations to the children of his first marriage? In one survey, reported in *Redbook* magazine, 30 percent of the second wives who responded said that financial responsibility toward their husband's first families makes it impossible for them to afford children of their own. Annie is bitter. "Art knew I wanted children and he led me to think before we were married that he would go along once we got settled. Now that I'm thirty-six, and time is running out, he's reneged. He says we just can't afford it."

Annie's bitterness about her own thwarted dreams doesn't help her attitude toward Art's children. Something seems to go wrong every time they visit. "Half the time they arrive without proper clothes," Annie complains, "and we have to buy pajamas, or jeans, or sneakers. Or they march in and say they need money for a school trip that their mother won't give them. It's just a never-ending drain."

There are many postdivorce money games, some of which center on the children and all of which can damage the new relationship. Sending children dressed in rags is just one version. Telling children that their noncustodial parent doesn't provide enough money is another. And then there are the former spouses who attack each other openly through the children. Pete, using business as an excuse, won't commit himself to regular visits; his child's mother and her new husband are therefore unable to make plans as a twosome. The stepfather, meanwhile, because he is available, bears the brunt of the child's anger at Pete.

Stepparents can get caught up in money games of their own. Uncertain of their new role, and not sure how to achieve a solid relationship with children they hardly know, they may seek to buy affection. It doesn't work. Set your stepchild up with a roomful of model trains, if you like, but don't expect the child to love you in return.

Don't be surprised, moreover, if the children themselves become manipulative in the wake of a parent's remarriage. As Linda Bird Francke points out in *Growing Up Divorced*, children and parents often establish a very special relationship after divorce. Remarriage means the loss of that special one-to-one relationship and the intrusion (in the child's eyes) of a stepparent. Some children withdraw when this happens. Some become more and more demanding, seeking material evidence that they are still loved.

Situation 3: As the plot thickens, we find two previously married partners, each with children; one set of children lives in, the other visits from time to time. Now we have two sets of children that have to get along with each other, as well as with a new stepparent, and two households with two sets of operating procedures. In one household, children may have strict limits set on what they spend; in the other, money may flow relatively freely. In one, children may be expected to work, while in the other handouts are the order of the day. In one, chores may be paid or misbehavior fined, in the other not.

These disparities can exist where income levels are similar. What happens when they're not? "It's very hard to visit back and forth on different economic levels," says Claire Berman, past president of the Stepfamily Association of America and author of *Making It As a Stepparent*. "How, for example, can a teenager refuse a trip to Europe? Yet accepting the trip builds up resentment among stepsiblings at home."

Some stepparents are willing to send stepchildren to Europe along with their own. Others draw the line, and sharply at that, when it comes to providing anything at all for someone else's child. As therapist Barbara Fishman wrote in the professional journal *Family Relations*, citing one family's pragmatic approach to this problem: "My ex-husband has money and he bought our son Ricky a car. That's great! But when my stepson David needs transportation, he is not permitted to borrow Ricky's car because my ex is adamant about not wanting to support someone else's child. Ricky would love to share the car with his stepbrother, but he can't risk angering his father. Besides, David is sensitive about being the 'poor' brother and would not drive it anyway." This family's solution: scraping together enough money to buy a secondhand car for David.

But pragmatic solutions aren't always readily available. What do you do when your stepchildren arrive dressed in designer originals while your own children wear hand-me-downs? You can't control the spending of your stepchildren's custodial parent, but you certainly can resent that spending. You can—and should—try not to let that resentment spill over on the children, but you'll be superhuman if you consistently succeed.

It's not very good for children to be used as weapons in adult wars. But it happens. In some reconstituted families one parent buys children goodies out of guilt, the other teaches them that they are entitled to financial advantages just because their parents are divorced, and a stepparent tries to be "better" than the natural parent by buying more things for the children. Who can possibly win? Not the children, who may well wind up "spoiled" in more ways than one, ill equipped for the real world they will have to inhabit.

A related problem exists when you, the stepparent, have gone all out to win over the children during your courtship. When the reality of daily life sets in after the marriage, when you start to act like a parent instead of a fairy godparent, the children "quite naturally," in Francke's words, "feel duped."

As children move among households, both the children themselves and their parents (biological and "step") face the potential for multilevel conflict. First of all, the stepparent and the resident children must get to know one another and establish a relationship. If it's the father who has custody and a stepmother who is home with his children, the relationship may be volatile. She wants to be a good mother but the children may not want her mothering at all. She's also not out earning an income if she's mothering full-time, so that her self-esteem may suffer. "I feel like nothing," Clara recalls. "His eight-year-old twins needed a mother but they didn't want that mother to be me; I couldn't do anything right as far as they were concerned. I'd given up my job so I had to ask Len for money; he'd question me about why I needed so much. It was a disaster. The only thing that saved us was my insistence on going back to school. I took courses while the boys were in day camp that summer and kept going when they returned to school. I feel like a person, in touch with other adults, and I'll be self-supporting again, at a higher level, by the time they're a few years older."

Sometimes money disrupts a tender new relationship between stepparent and stepchildren. Sometimes the issue is discipline. A child may yell, "You have no right to tell me what to do; you're not my father." The natural parent may also reject your attempts at discipline, protectively hovering over the child. At the same time, says Bohannan, "Social scientists who have studied stepchildren find a correlation between their view of whether the stepparent loves them and whether the stepparent makes them behave. 'He doesn't make me mind, therefore he doesn't love me' is their complaint." Establishing authority can't be rushed, but it must happen. Just be prepared to thrash out the issue with your spouse, perhaps repeatedly, before the issue is resolved.

The resident children must also get to know and establish some sort of relationship with the visiting children who, in turn, must get to know the other parent. All this is hard enough if the newlyweds have set up residence in a new household. When you've moved into a home previously occupied by one of you and his or her children, the situation gets even stickier. In this case, one set of children may feel as if the new stepparent is invading their turf while the parent, in turn, needs time to feel truly at home.

Meanwhile, there may be (and often are) financial pressures from the first spouse of either or both parents. The pressures may be chronic, as in the need to make regular child support payments. They may also be acute, as when an "ex" requests extra money: The kids need music lessons or new winter coats or whatever. A continual flow of such requests can put a strain on the best of second marriages. Glynnis Walker, the author of *Second Wife, Second Best?* and a second wife herself, notes that wives and even children can be very good at extracting money by playing on a man's guilt about the failure of his first marriage. Her advice to second wives: Help your husband understand that he's not doing them a favor by not letting them stand on their own two feet.

But it isn't that easy. Both men and women, rightly or wrongly, often do feel guilty when a marriage fails. Those guilt feelings can be used manipulatively, with more or less success, by a former spouse. Sometimes, of course, the money just isn't there and whether you want to provide extras for your first children out of guilt or simply because you love them, you may not be able to do so. How much *do* you owe to your first set of children? to your new spouse's children? to that new spouse and to yourself?

Look at the remarried man, cited by sociologist Lenore J. Weitzman in *The Marriage Contract*, who is legally obligated to support three children, two from a former marriage and one from his current marriage. He has no legal obligation to his new wife's two children from her former marriage, because he has not legally adopted them, but because they are living in his household he finds that he is contributing to their support. What's worse, his wife's ex-husband, who has remarried and started a new family, has stopped paying court-ordered child support. "Our man," says Weitzman, "feels the law should either relieve him of his financial obligation to support his own two children by his ex-wife (who are now living in another man's household) or force his present wife's ex-husband to pay his support obligations. He is disconcerted to learn that there are no legal guidelines to allocate and apportion support responsibilities among several families."

When there are legal guidelines, to the chagrin of some observers, they may extend even beyond a second divorce. Court rulings in some states have held that a divorced stepfather who had assumed financial responsibility for stepchildren during his marriage to their mother must pay child support after the marriage dissolves. Usually, but not always, such responsibility is limited to stepparents who have legally adopted their stepchildren.

And all this concerns the practical considerations! Just think of the emotional fallout that must inevitably result: Wife No. 2, during an intact second marriage, feels guilty about the money her new husband is spending on her children. At the same time she resents the money he sends to support his first family, but is angry at her ex-husband for not caring about his own children. Money isn't just money. It represents love when it's given, and hostility when it's withheld. Wife No. 2 is glad, despite her guilt, that her new husband provides for her children; it shows her that he cares. She resents his support of his first family, at the same time, because she'd rather those ties diminished. And she's angry at her own first husband, as irrational as it may seem, because he should love his children and prove that love by sending money. It is most certainly a tangled web we weave.

Situation 4: When the children in a "blended" family are still fairly young they will adapt, given plenty of time, to the new family constellation. When they are older at the time their parents remarry, both more set in their ways and ready to break loose from the family, the process may be more difficult. Let's look at a family with "his" and "hers" sets of teenagers plus a new baby of their own.

Both sets of teenagers live in this new household, which, in itself, sets up potential conflict. Recent research findings have some interesting things to say about the importance of birth order in determining personality and behavior. What happens, then, when birth order "changes" relatively late in life as the result of a parent's remarriage? Jerry was 16, the oldest of three, when his father married for the second time. Jerry's stepmother also had three children and all three were older than Jerry. In one sense this was good, because two of the three were already away at school and hence not permanently part of the new household. But 17-year-old Jennifer, the youngest in her original family and now the eldest, was very much on the scene. Jerry and Jenny both had new roles to learn; neither enjoyed the switch although neither understood why.

The teen years are difficult for all concerned. Adolescents, by definition, are becoming independent. That process is never easy, even in an "intact" family, and often results in a psychological push-and-pull that can drive parents to distraction. When one resident parent is a stepparent, especially a relatively recent stepparent, he or she may feel personally rejected. Just remember: Attempts to pressure an adolescent into a closely loving relationship will probably backfire. And it's vitally important, for the sake of your marriage as well as the children, to present a united parental front on important issues. While children benefit from seeing differing parental views and seeing how you reach decisions, they are also adept at manipulation. If you let them see you divided on major matters, you shouldn't be surprised if the children (no matter how old they are) try to drive a wedge between you and break up your marriage.

On the practical financial front, as if psychological warfare isn't bad enough, there are also problems. Spending habits of adolescents may be difficult to alter, even in the face of financial reality, especially if a hormone-laden adolescent blames that reality on the stepparent. "I could have had a car for graduation, if Dad hadn't married *her*," a disgruntled teenager may claim, conveniently disregarding the fact that his own mother had expected him to earn at least part of the cost. If the stepmother's child gets a car from *his* father, of course, tensions will escalate.

And then there's college, looming relentlessly on the horizon. Now that the legal age of majority is 18 in most states, child support usually stops at 18 (unless agreement has been made to the contrary). This leaves the other parent, together with his or her new spouse, in a tremendous financial bind. Student aid may not even be available because college financial aid offices often look at the resources of both parent and stepparent in determining eligibility, without regard to the stepparent's legal liability, ability to pay, or willingness to pay.

Financial pressures on the parents can lead to emotional strain as well. But the effect on the child may be shattering. "Children's taken-for-granted expectations about the future are often altered by the divorce," Weitzman writes in *The Divorce Revolution*, as children lose the college education (or, at least, the *kind* of college education) they've been promised. She cites the case of a young man whose father had always pressed him to follow in the paternal footsteps at Dartmouth; after the divorce the same father said that private college was out of the question and the boy would have to live at home and commute to a state college. "While this father could still 'afford' to send his son to Dartmouth, his priorities had changed." Where there is a stepfather at hand, the teen may still hope for the college education of his dreams. But the stepfather, much as he might like to provide that education, may not have the resources or, if he does, may feel that those resources must be saved for his own children.

Sometimes grandparents step in to help with college. And sometimes, for the children of divorce, those grandparents may be from the first family. This sets up emotional pressures on another dimension. "I always wanted the boys to stay close to their first grandparents," as one mother says, "but it's become increasingly uncomfortable. Sometimes I feel as if we're being blackmailed— so much visitation in exchange for help with college or a mention in their will."

Children do benefit, however, from having loving grandparents and this may be one instance where it really is the more, the merrier. "My parents are thrilled to have more grandchildren—they never wanted me to stop at two with my first wife, and they're ecstatic because Stacey has three of her own. They've 'adopted' her kids, and lavish them with presents as much as they do mine. Sometimes I think they're spoiling all five!"

That new baby on the scene, just as everybody was getting to know one another, introduces another element. New babies, just because they're babies, take a lot of time and attention. Older children, even when they're full brothers and sisters, can feel left out. They also feel the additional consequences of birth-order rearrangement; a youngest, for example, may feel both displaced and delighted at no longer being the "baby" of the family. When those older children are stepsiblings they may feel like characters in *Cinderella*. I don't mean to imply a wicked stepmother or, for that matter, stepfather. But a proud new parent may devote financial resources to the child of the new union that are not available to either set of children from previous unions. Grandparents, too, may get caught up in the thrill of a new life, sometimes showing such favoritism to their "own" grandchild that the stepgrandchildren feel cruelly rejected. The more extended the family, the more convoluted the scenario can become.

Grandparents run into emotional rapids as well. "Our daughter and her new husband each have a child by a previous marriage; he has legally adopted her daughter.

We love both children, but we're wrestling with what to do with our wills. What's fair? Do we leave everything divided between the two grandchildren? What if this marriage doesn't work out?" This grandfather faces a real dilemma. A possible solution might be to leave the money to the daughter and let her, in turn, decide what to do for her child and stepchild. It may mean higher estate taxes—a good tax attorney should be consulted—but the peace of mind may make it all worthwhile.

Situation 5: After all the complexity of life-with-children, it may look as if late-life remarriage with no resident children is a cup of tea. Well, not quite. Granted, older folk (in a first marriage or a second) have the privacy and the freedom, and usually the funds, to enjoy life of their own choosing. But that doesn't mean that there are no problems at all. You and your new partner may have different expectations, which should be worked out in advance. Adult children, moreover, don't necessarily take kindly to the notion of a parent's remarriage. If you have substantial assets, your children may come right out and suggest that your new love is after your money. If the remarriage takes place after one parent's death, whether or not assets are substantial, the adult child may feel happy that you've found companionship but at the same time threatened by a new alliance. There may be fears, expressed or not, about losing a rightful inheritance. You can ease those fears by discussing your plans and any changes in your will with your grown children.

If the remarriage takes place after divorce, the feelings are once again more complicated. Recent studies have shown that there is no good time, as far as children are concerned, for their parents to divorce. Men and women in their twenties, thirties, and even forties find their world made suddenly more insecure by their parents' divorce. Later, they may be equally upset by the prospect of remarriage. That doesn't mean that you must stick with an unhappy marriage, or forgo remarriage, for the sake of children who are already out on their own. But it does mean that you should be aware of their likely feelings, and you should try to discuss the issue openly.

It won't necessarily be easy. Multiple marriages are creating "a period of interfamily feuds the likes of which you have never seen," Connecticut attorney William Selsberg told *The New York Times*. "Who is entitled to get college money if there isn't enough to go around? How do you equitably settle the claims of the children from the different marriages when the parent dies? What if the children from a former marriage are left out of the will? Estate planning is becoming impossible."

Premarital Agreements

When remarrying partners have adult children as well as property amassed over the years, a premarital (sometimes called prenuptial or antenuptial) agreement is definitely in order. An agreement also makes sense where children are young but one or both partners brings property to the marriage, or expects to receive property through inheritance that they would like passed on to their own children.

Premarital agreements are legally recognized in most states. Just don't include trivia, such as who will do the dishes, if you want your agreement to stick. Don't include sexual matters, such as the right to experimentation outside of marriage. And don't try to put something over on your partner, or the agreement won't hold up. Ralph asked Mary, just a day or two before their wedding, to sign a simple agreement providing that each relinquished all claims to the other's estate. But the estates were disproportionate. When Ralph died, leaving an estate of $640,000 (to Mary's $15,000), she realized that she had given up too much. The court agreed, on the grounds that (1) Mary was unaware of the extent of Ralph's assets and (2) there was an element of coercion in presenting her with an agreement to sign when wedding arrangements had already been made.

A Uniform Premarital Agreement Act has been introduced by the National Conference of Commissioners on

Uniform State Laws and endorsed by the American Bar Association. By the close of 1985 the act had been adopted in just three states: Virginia, North Dakota, and California. It's worth looking at, though, because Uniform Law proposals tend to influence state law even when they are not adopted on a word-for-word basis. The Uniform Premarital Agreement Act is very simple. It defines the agreement as one made in contemplation of marriage, states that it must be in writing and signed by both parties, becoming effective upon the marriage of the parties. It specifies that both parties must agree voluntarily, and that each must fully understand the property and financial obligations of the other. The content is up to the parties, although the act does list certain items which *may* be included, such as the right to manage and control property; the disposition of property upon separation, divorce, or death; the modification or elimination of spousal support; the ownership in life insurance.

If you plan a premarital agreement, therefore, be sure to fully disclose all your assets. Then see an attorney, preferably a separate attorney for each of you, and draw up your agreement well in advance of the wedding. Make sure that you understand all the implications. You might agree to transfer a life insurance policy to your new partner, for example, so that he or she can control the beneficiary designation; that transfer, depending on the value of the policy, may have gift-tax implications.

While some remarrying couples refuse to consider a premarital agreement—"it erodes the trust in a marital relationship," according to an Ohio woman who speaks for many—working through the details of an agreement can clear the air, forestalling later quarrels. Moreover, you and your partner have complete control over the terms of your agreement. You can word it so that it phases in additional support for your new spouse with additional years of marriage. You can work it so that it self-destructs after a specified period of time. Or you can simply agree to review it later on and either revise or revoke it then. Like a will, in other words, a premarital agreement can be changed when you, as a team, choose to do so. Like a will, the contents of your premarital agreement—or, at least, the fact that you have made one—should be discussed with your adult children.

Merger Time

In many ways, says therapist Fishman, the merger of two families is like a corporate merger. "The stepfamily merger, like the business merger, is built upon its previous economy and history—e.g., the finances of the first marriage and divorce settlements. People who marry young, in first marriages, become adults together and in the process develop an interdependent economic life. Although financial issues may cause conflict, the marriage itself is most often a single economic unit, supported by either one or both partners. A second marriage is different. . . . A major task for the newly remarried couple is to merge two disparate economies into a cooperative financial organization which will be different from anything they have previously experienced."

Fishman goes on to develop her "one-pot," "two-pot" theory of economic behavior in blended families. The "one-pot" economy is based on the common good, with assets distributed in accordance with the need of family members; both husband and wife earn income and that income is handled jointly, for the benefit of all. In the "two-pot" economy, biological identity is more important than need as each parent cares first for his or her own children. Each model can work; which one you adopt may depend on your personal financial style (would you be likely, in a first marriage for each, to pool your income or keep it separate?), how much income you each have, and the source of that income.

When there is little, if any, money from outside sources—child support is erratic, if it comes at all—you are more likely to pool your resources and act as a single economic unit. This is particularly true if you feel economically hard-pressed, without money to spare, and must use all your available funds to make ends meet. But it's also a matter of attitude, of commitment to the new relationship. Even with commitment, however, choices are not always easy for the blended family. You may be willing to foot the bills for your stepdaughter's college education, but how do you feel when it means you have to postpone buying a computer for your business? You may be willing to pay for that same stepdaughter's wedding, but how will you feel when she walks down the aisle on her "real" dad's arm?

The questions are different when you don't pool your resources, instead choosing to contribute specific amounts to your joint household while separately supporting your own children. Separate funds make life a lot easier, in the opinion of many stepfamily experts; without separate funds there can be power struggles and a tough time negotiating who spends what on whose kids. Yet there's less commitment with this arrangement, Fishman found, as well as more continuing involvement with ex-spouses and their families. That involvement can lead to mixed emotions. How do you feel, in this scenario, when your partner's former in-laws pay for your stepchildren's college education? You might feel relieved of the financial burden. Or you might feel that these voices from the past are haunting your new marriage.

Studies show that remarriages have less longevity than first marriages; 60 percent end in divorce, with more than 40 percent ending in divorce within five years. That divorce is more likely to occur when both partners have children from a previous marriage. "Indications are that remarried couples without children have the highest chance for success," Frances Klagsbrun notes in *Married People: Staying Together in the Age of Divorce*, "followed by those with grown children and those with children only of their own marriage. Marriages that include children from one spouse's previous marriage rank next, and those with children from both their previous marriages have the least promising outlook." The more configurations in the family landscape, not surprisingly, the greater the complications.

But there are ways to ease the complications. It takes good will on both sides, but we'll assume motivation to make the new marriage work. It takes understanding and open communication. And it takes attention to practical details.

Understanding starts, ideally, before marriage. While previously married courting couples, like any courting couples, are unlikely to be much interested in discussing the financial facts of life, it is extremely harmful to play ostrich. Ignoring existing obligations and refusing to consider future obligations is a head-in-the-sand approach to matrimony that won't work. These are some of the things you should discuss:

• *Alimony and child support.* If you are required to pay, how will the endless outgo affect your ability to support a new family? If your new spouse will have to earn income on an ongoing basis, that should be clear at the outset. If you won't be able to see your way clear to having more children, that should also be clear. If you are on the receiving end of alimony, it will probably stop with your remarriage. Child support, if you are lucky, will continue. How will you handle those payments? Will you keep them separate, applied toward your children's health and welfare, or will you pool the money and apply it toward the well-being of your entire new family?

• *Visitation schedules and custody arrangements.* The schedules arranged as single parents may have to be modified if either you or your former spouse remarry. Can you work together well enough to make arrangements in the best interests of the children? Can you be at all flexible? Discuss current arrangements with your new partner, and be sure he or she understands your legal and emotional commitment to your children.

• *Expectations for your respective children.* What role do you want your new partner to play in rearing your children? Will you back him or her in the effort to play that role? What about your own relationship with your partner's children? It may be impossible to anticipate just what will happen after you all live together, but do your best and reach some mutual conclusions.

• *Fringe benefits.* If you have agreed to maintain your first spouse as beneficiary of your life insurance, or keep intact a former mate's share of your pension, be sure your new partner understands and accepts the arrangement.

• *Existing assets.* If you have retained the family home after your divorce, for example, will you want that home to be left directly to your children? Does that mean your spouse will have to move out at your death? See below on structuring wills and trusts to accomplish your aims but do be sure, at the outset, that your new partner understands and agrees with those aims.

• *Existing debts.* If one of you owes sizable sums, will the other be willing to assume any responsibility? Or will you agree to keep separate obligations separate, even if it means you come into marriage on an unequal footing?

• *Newly acquired property.* As you acquire property in your new marriage, how will that property be owned? Will you be willing to put things in both names? Find out how you *both* feel about this, before the marriage takes place. And try to understand if your partner has some misgivings about joint ownership, as you will want your partner to be understanding if you are the one to hold back; when someone has been hurt by divorce, it may take time to fully trust again.

• *The income you will earn,* from any source (wages, interest, dividends, royalties, etc.) after your marriage. How will you handle that income? Are you willing to have the fruits of your labor support your stepchildren? Does it make any difference whether or not those children live with you? What about your own children and their stepparent?

• *In-laws and the extended family.* What kind of ties do you hope or expect to maintain with relatives from your first marriage? Is it important to you that your children keep in touch with all their grandparents? (If not, you may break a couple of hearts, as well as shortchange your children.) What about aunts and uncles and cousins? Lives can be enriched by extended families, or confused by mixed feelings toward a multiplicity of relationships. It is, at least in part, up to you.

Estate Planning

As you discuss and determine the ins and outs of your new relationship, you should take steps to allocate your property after death. You should each write a will (reviewing and replacing, as necessary, any previous will) to protect both your first family and your second. If you don't write a will—and seven out of ten people, it's been estimated, die without one—you'll lose any say over who receives your hard-earned assets. The laws of your state will step in and dictate the distribution.

Think carefully about what you want to do, and discuss your intentions with your spouse. As a single parent, for example, you may have willed all of your property to your children. You may, in your new marriage, want to continue this arrangement. Fair enough, as long as your spouse understands and agrees (and, of course, is otherwise provided for). Your spouse has a legal right to a portion of your estate, typically one-third where there are children and one-half where there are no children. The waiver of that right is a standard part of a premarital agreement. But you may both agree to a waiver and still provide for each other.

If your assets are sizable, you might want to consider the use of a trust. A so-called Q-Tip trust (technically, a qualified terminal interest property trust) pemits a spouse to leave interest income from the trust to a spouse during his or her lifetime while leaving the principal of the trust to other beneficiaries. The surviving spouse can't change the beneficiary, so it's a way of ensuring that spouse's financial well-being while leaving the money itself to your children. Normally, I don't believe in tying a spouse's hands by setting up an irrevocable trust (see Chapter 9) but, in this situation, a Q-Tip trust can protect both spouse and children.

Just be sure that you understand the ramifications of your arrangements, whether in a simple will or a complex trust. Otherwise it could be *your* child writing the following letter to an advice columnist:

> My father married my stepmother two years ago. She got one-third of the estate when he died. The other two-thirds is "in trust" for my brother and me, but she will collect the interest as long as she lives and we can't touch it. When she dies, the money is ours.
>
> My children need that money for their schooling. Her grandson is going through college on interest from our estate! And there is nothing we can do, as his will is legal.

The complexities of financial relationships in a second marriage continue after the death of one or both participants. The father in the above case failed to think ahead. If there was enough money to divide, and to leave two-thirds in trust, there was also enough to make an outright grant to his children. His children may have been delighted that he found a second loving relationship, but their delight is no more.

It doesn't take major assets, or irrevocable trusts, to upset the financial/emotional applecart. Perhaps the most valuable thing you own is the family home. You hung on to it after the divorce, with great difficulty, and you want your children to have it after you're gone. There's just one problem. The family home is now your new spouse's home as well. Do you want that spouse to be faced with virtually simultaneous loss of a loving partner *and* a home? This unfortunate scenario can take place even if you bought the house together and own it together, if your wills each leave all your assets to your respective children. Then, notes California attorney Nancy Boxley Tepper, the house might have to be sold before the assets can be distributed to the children. Unless your spouse can afford to buy out your half, he or she will have to leave.

Some possible solutions: Will the house to your children, with a proviso that your widow(er) has a lifetime right of occupancy. Have the house held in trust for the surviving spouse for a designated period of time, after which it will be sold and the proceeds distributed in accordance with your will. Or, if all of you (parent, stepparent and children) have complete faith in one another, simply leave the house to your spouse with the understanding that either the house itself or the proceeds from its sale will be left to your children in your spouse's will.

There are alternative solutions to most problems. Finding the right solution means taking the time to think it through, and to discuss it with all the people most closely involved.

Money Traps for the Remarried

• The tangled feelings and tangled finances of the blended family require extra doses of patience and understanding. Don't expect immediate trust and an immediate merger of assets. And don't expect children to accept the new relationship right away; it may take several years.

• Remaining on good terms with the extended family of previous and current marriages may be desirable but difficult. If money rears its head, a new spouse's (understandable) sensitivity may make these extended relationships intolerable.

• Your spouse may be torn between commitments to two families. If so, your overt resentment of those commitments—even if they place an unbearable burden on your pocketbook—will not help. State your case as objectively as you can, but try to understand that you may be in a situation where nobody can truly win.

· 7 ·

Parenthood

CHILDREN ADD a fascinating and sometimes frustrating ingredient to the money equation. Where once you were two, agreeing or disagreeing on how to spend and save, now you are three; that third isn't going to argue with you about the spending of money, not for several years at least, but is going to be responsible for spending a great deal. What's more, while you may have thought that your respective attitudes toward money were well sorted out before baby made three, you may now find new issues coming to the surface and demanding resolution.

A child may help you to focus your financial efforts and lead you to plan your financial future. A child may also generate a pocketbook crunch. If you resolve the cash shortfall by remaining a two-income household, you may find problems revolving around child care, parental leave, and an overwhelming feeling that life is simply too much. If you cope with child-rearing by becoming a full-time parent, giving up one income, the parent who stops earning may detect a shift in the balance of power within the family.

How will you meet the challenge of paying for eighteen years of child-rearing? What will you do about combining an outside job with inside parenting? How will you resolve your own feelings about status and security in a one-income household?

When an Income Stops

Combine the costs of child-rearing with the loss of one income, and you let yourself in for trauma with a capital

T. The quarter-million-dollar baby (we'll tackle the specifics of child-rearing costs a bit later in this chapter) is a tremendous burden for one parent to sustain alone. Single parents don't have much choice. And many two-parent families elect to get along on one income, at least on a temporary basis. That's because the alternative, in our society today, isn't easy either. Women, even if they work full-time outside the home, still maintain most of the responsibility for housekeeping and child-rearing . . . and Superwomen, despite media hype, are as hard to come by as Supermen. Corporate America doesn't encourage parents—fathers *or* mothers—to put children first. Government certainly doesn't support the notion of readily available and affordable child care. And mothers themselves, even if they've planned a short maternity leave and a quick trip back to the job, often change their minds when confronted with the helpless dependence of a small baby.

There's no arguing, at least not from this quarter, that raising children is an important job and one that needs to be done well. But raising children, like maintaining a home, is not a job that is materially rewarded in our society. When jobs are not materially rewarding, unfortunately, they frequently lead to lessened self-esteem. "The fact that a woman is not bringing in money, which she did for years," states the Langer Report on *The New Mature Mother*, "has a dramatic effect on the way she spends and on her self-image." Even women who have worked for years suddenly feel that they can't spend money they haven't earned and that they are somehow lessened by not earning. That deflated sense of self-worth is nurtured by husbands who equate income with power. (While I've tried to be gender-neutral throughout this book, this particular stereotype is still all too true.)

"Money has a lot to do with the balance of power in our marriage," is the way a New Jersey woman puts it. "He was in law school and I was teaching when we got married. We had a full partnership then, sharing housework as well as money. That partnership lasted for seven years, until our first child was born and I stayed home. Before, decisions were made jointly. Then, he became the breadwinner. *He* wanted a sports car, *he* was earning the money, *he* bought the car. We were planning to buy a house, but all of a sudden that didn't matter. He called me a parasite. He asked what right I had to reap the benefits of his working." This woman, in the process of securing a divorce, adds: "I wouldn't marry again without working. Men don't respect women who don't earn."

The bitterness of a failed marriage inflames this woman's memories of her marriage and her feelings about earning money. Divorce has a way of doing that. Within an intact marriage, husbands and wives may agree on a division of labor—he earns, she manages—during the time when children are small. Once they've agreed, they may insist that there's no problem at all when it comes to money. But there are undercurrents. "I don't spend too much," Nancy says. "Actually I feel more guilty about spending money. I'm not really working so maybe that's why. But," she sidesteps, "I'm not really guilty." A skittishness about spending showed up in interview after interview with one-income couples. Sometimes it was a full-time mother who shied away from spending. Sometimes it was a husband who objected to a wife's spending. "It took a little bit of education," as one Indiana man put it, "but I've redirected her thinking about spending."

That redirection is often a shift toward spending on family and children instead of on self. "Whenever there's money that I'm going to spend," said a respondent to the Langer survey, "it's more likely to be spent on the house or the husband and kid rather than me because I didn't make it so I shouldn't spend it on myself." That redirection is also toward dependency. "We have to turn around after being independent and say 'Could I have?' You want something and it isn't that you're asking for a new blouse or a new pair of shoes or stockings. It's that you know you're going to be with the baby and the stores are probably right there and if you had the money you could dart right in and get whatever it is. I find that my husband has a very hard time with that. Not that he doesn't want to give me the money. It's like all of a sudden I have to explain what I want. I have to let him know a day ahead of time and I have to tell him what it's for." It's the asking that's so difficult for women who are used to being independent.

In sociological terms, the earning wife is generally a junior partner in marriage (relatively few are full partners). Her husband's role as breadwinner is paramount, but, because she is contributing to the family welfare, she has a voice in how money is spent. As sociologists Letha Dawson Scanzoni and John Scanzoni put it in *Men, Women & Change,* "she may point out the unfairness of her husband's insistence on making huge expenditures without consulting her, particularly when she knows such expenditures would be impossible without her contributions to the family income. Or on the other hand, she might object to her husband's nagging about the price of something she purchased—even though it was purchased out of her own earnings rather than out of some 'allowance' from him . . ." When a wife earns income, in short, she has a share in family decision-making. When she does not, she frequently reverts to a subsidiary non-partner role.

This shift can take place at the highest income levels. Doris was international director of financial operations for a major pharmaceuticals company, earning over $50,000 a year, when she decided to stay home full-time with her 6-month-old daughter. After never being financially dependent on her husband in ten years of marriage, she says, "That was one of the hardest things, being dependent on him, on his income and his health." Her husband earns a handsome income, and the family did not suffer a financial trauma when Doris left her job. But she felt the difference in her own status.

Delayed Parenthood

Doris didn't reach her $50,000-plus salary at the age of 22; like many women today, she delayed parenthood

until her career was well established. Census Bureau
data confirm that more and more women are delaying
childbirth until their mid or late thirties. Childlessness
is now at uncommonly high levels among women in their
twenties, while the birth rate is rising among women in
their thirties and forties. Where fewer than one-quarter
of married women between the ages of 20 and 24 didn't
have children in 1960, fully 43 percent of the married
women in this age bracket in 1982 had no children. Some
never will have children; others will join the mini-baby
boom of the thirties generation.

Babies born to older parents enter a different home
environment. Their parents are more likely to be college
educated, to have higher incomes, and to hold profes-
sional-level jobs. Their parents are used to a degree of
self-indulgence; with two incomes they've been able to
buy many of the good things in life. When a baby is born,
especially if one income stops, self-indulgence may have
to stop as well. New parents stay at home more, sharply
cutting back on eating out and entertainment. They pick
up on these activities again within a few months or a
year but, in the interim, devote their energies—and
their pocketbooks—to the younger generation. Older
parents, studies show, spend more on their children.
They do so partly because they have more money than
younger couples. And they do so because it gives them
great pleasure. "Before, we were impulse buyers," says
an Illinois woman, "buying a lot of gadgets. When we
buy gadgets now, they're for the kids. We get such a
kick out of buying for them."

Yet many new parents, husbands in particular, seem
to be unprepared for the expenses of parenthood. Some
resent them. One father comments: "I notice we're not
able to save as much. [Money] is going out for things it
never was before, like milk and bottles and diapers and
on and on. It's harder to save and that's important." This
same man, remarking on changes that have taken place
since the baby was born and his wife left her newspaper
job, says that he'd like to curb what he views as his wife's

impulse buying. "Women are always being bombarded with messages to change the style of their clothes, purses, shoes, etc. and so they go out and buy on impulse."

Older parents may have deliberately postponed parenthood in order to gain a solid financial footing, but a shift in that financial footing provokes uneasiness. It isn't that "Yuppie-dom" is hard to give up, but that both the life-style and the balance of power can (and frequently do) change with the birth of the first child. Regular dining out of a two-income couple gives way, in almost a symbolic sense, to at-home meals timed to a child's eating and sleeping routine. Shared decision-making gives way, imperceptibly, to breadwinner dominance. It's a major adjustment.

Loss of power seems to go with loss of income, even in the most egalitarian of couples, without regard to whose idea it is that a mother stay at home. "I wasn't planning to quit my job when Jenny was born, but when Don was transferred to Houston it seemed simpler all around for me to be a full-time mother for a couple of years. I hadn't realized how powerless I would feel when I had no income of my own. Don says there's no problem, but he just doesn't see all the subtle ways he uses money to assert control. I'll have to take a job soon, even if the housekeeper makes more than I do, just to become a full human being."

The conflicts are legion. Perhaps *she* wants to return to work, while *he* thinks her place is in the home. Or *she* wants to stay home; *he* is counting the days until she can return to work and bring in some income. Or *they* both want her at home, but can't afford to have her stay there. "It's the house payments that are the killer," says a husband in this situation. "We wanted to buy a house before we had a baby, but it takes two incomes to support the house."

It may also take two incomes, well into the future, to support the costs of child-rearing. Parents who delayed childbearing may find themselves paying college tuition in the years when they should be preparing for their own retirement. Don't expect the crunch to ease, in other words; it may only get worse.

The Costs of Child-rearing

Precious bundles, as any parent knows, cost precious bucks. But it's easy to underestimate the overwhelming costs of child-rearing. Just to give you pause, before breaking down the figures, look at a round number in the neighborhood of a quarter of a million dollars.

Exactly how much you will spend depends on the number of children you have, where you live, your socio-economic status, and the wife's employment status. The most important factor, according to Thomas J. Espenshade, an economist who has made extensive studies of the cost of child-rearing, is the number of children you have. As with other purchases the per-item cost goes down when you buy in bulk.

Children aren't groceries, of course, and we don't decide how many we'll have on the basis of unit cost. But economists have estimated that raising one child absorbs about a quarter of a family's lifetime income. A little thought given to all the direct and indirect expenditures involved in raising children is clearly in order; it will enable you to plan ahead and it might even preclude some parent-to-parent conflict.

Economists consider the costs of rearing children in terms of both direct maintenance costs and what they call "opportunity" costs. The direct costs are all those out-of-pocket dollars that mount up from the moment a child is born until the day that child turns eighteen (college costs come later, add considerably more). Opportunity costs are less tangible but no less real: They are losses of opportunities for economic betterment, opportunities often lost when working women become full-time mothers.

Mothers who go right back to work after a paid maternity leave may not suffer reduced income, although they will face higher direct outlays for child care, but mothers who drop out of the labor force for several years forgo both current income and career advancement. An average of $45,355 is "lost" when a new mother who was working part-time and earning just $5.60 an hour stays home until her child is 14 years old. With inflation over that fourteen-year period, and a perhaps more realistic pay scale of $8 an hour, according to Espenshade, the loss of income ranges from almost $74,000 to $108,000. Full-time and higher-paid workers, especially professional and managerial women, lose a great deal more. Exact figures are hard to come by, but one estimate of lost earnings for a woman with postgraduate education stands at half a million dollars—or about one-third of her anticipated lifetime income.

The money spent on child-rearing, moreover, whether a wife stops working or not, is not available for spending on other things, on either an enhanced life-style or on investments for the future. A housewife's labors have been estimated to be "worth" at least $7 an hour but that is money it would cost her family in her absence, not money that she brings in. With lower income and greater outgo, expectations have to be lowered.

Direct Costs

Opportunity costs may be hard to calculate. Direct costs are all too evident. They start with the costs of delivery (about $3,000, these days, for an uncomplicated delivery; add another $1,000 or so for the increasingly frequent cesarean section) and end with the high school graduation party (frankfurters and Coke . . . or a catered affair). These direct economic costs for an urban child born in the North Central United States in 1984, as calculated by the U.S. Department of Agriculture, come to $140,927. That's until age 18. At that point you can add in another $30,000 to $60,000 for college.

These government estimates, many people believe, are low. Uncle Sam allocates $142 for clothing, for example, in the first year of a child's life. Granted, infants don't wear very much. They also receive a lot of gifts. But spend $10 a week for disposable diapers, add in some bibs and blankets, and there goes not only the $142 for clothing but the entire $579 allocated for "other expenses." By the time your child is a teenager, and "needs" Adidas sneakers and Calvin Klein jeans, the yearly USDA clothing allocation is over $900—but $900 doesn't buy much in these status-conscious and fast-growing years. Then there's education. Children from ages 1 through 5 stay ignorant, Uncle Sam says, but a 6-year-old may spend $166 a year on educational pursuits. Have you tried providing gymnastics for $166 a year? Or weekly piano lessons? There goes the "other expenses" allocation of $812.

There is no provision at all for child care in government estimates, and, as we shall see, child care can be a major part of your budget. And there's no mention of life insurance, which you will probably acquire in order to safeguard your child's future, or of investments on behalf of your child. On the other hand, your infant probably doesn't require much in the way of food, transportation, or housing—at least not until you decide that you need a bigger house for your growing family. Taken all in all, $250,000 from birth to age 18 is probably a modest estimate.

The outlay doesn't come all at once, fortunately, and it should be considered in terms of your overall family financial cycle. The birth year has some sizable expenditures, then expenses subside for about five years before heading steadily upward. Income, meanwhile, tends to continue rising (barring one income earner's temporarily "stopping out" of the work force) through the child-rearing years, then remains relatively stable from the middle years until retirement. The peak of outgo, associated with the growing family, frequently occurs ten full years earlier than the peak of income. This translates into a budgetary crunch in your children's teen years and a period of diminished discretionary spending. This period of mid-life marriage will be discussed in Chapter 8—but looking ahead can pave the way.

You don't calculate dollars-and-cents when you decide to have a child. But those dollars-and-cents can generate some conflict if you're not prepared. How do you feel about spending money on your pride and joy? And does your spouse feel the same way? Will a freshly painted hand-me-down crib suit the purpose? Or must Junior have the latest model? In an era when designer-label crib sheets on New York's Madison Avenue can run to hundreds of dollars, there are many temptations to spend. From silver rattle to sports car, from the first allowance to the last tuition bill, you'll find lots of opportunity for discussion of child-centered spending.

Combining Child-rearing with Career

One of the earliest discussions may center about whether or not the mother of an infant should return to her outside job. It's a tough question. Most people assume that working mothers must feel guilty about leaving young children in order to pursue their careers. Many do. But a recent study conducted at United States International University in San Diego indicates that mothers who stay at home experience more guilt than those who work.

Some homemakers feel guilty about staying home and not contributing to the family's income. Some are sensitive to undercurrents of criticism; "I'm not 'fulfilling my potential,' " one says sarcastically, "if all I do is raise a decent human being." Others who gave up careers to stay home after their children were born found it difficult to deal with negative feelings they previously held themselves about wives who stayed home. "They thought that women who stayed home were 'flakes,' " says Janet Murphy, the marriage and family therapist who conducted the San Diego study, "and so therefore now that they were staying home they wondered if they had become flakes as well." Women who move from paying jobs to nonpaying motherhood also suffer from what Dr. Mur-

phy calls "identity confusion." "The nonworking mother
sometimes loses the sense of who she is. She sees herself
as either the wife of someone or the mother of someone.
She finds it harder to maintain her own identity."

Some women return to the work force to salvage a
sense of self-worth. Many do so for the sake of the income
they can earn, even if virtually all of that income will be
spent on the children. Some, at higher income levels,
do so for the sake of added purchasing power above and
beyond basic living costs. "It's important to me that my
children dress well, that they have music lessons and
gymnastics and can go to camp. We can't do all this unless
I work." In the words of the Langer Report, their "expectations are high and carry an expensive price tag. While
in the past it would have been the husband's role to
support this lifestyle, or the couple would have reduced
their standard of living, today most of the working mothers studied felt they should and are expected to share
this responsibility." Most working fathers feel the same
way.

If you return to the work force shortly after your child
is born, whether you feel guilty about doing so or not,
you'll have lots of company. The Bureau of Labor Statistics reports that between 1973 and 1983 the labor force
participation rate for married women with school-age
children rose by 14 percentage points, to a total of 68
percent. For wives with children under age 6, the rate
rose from 33 to 50 percent. By March 1984, nearly half
of all mothers of infants and toddlers under the age of 3
were in the labor force; in 1970 just 30 percent of the
mothers in this category were working outside the home.

Of the 32 million children with mothers holding paying
jobs, 27 percent are solely supported by their mothers;
the fathers are either "absent," unemployed, or not in
the labor force. In the rest of the families where mothers
earn, those mothers make an important contribution to
total family income. For all two-parent families with children, median 1982 income was $30,030 when the mother
worked and $23,900 when she did not. Women, like

men, work for many reasons. But the statistics, in the words of Janet L. Norwood, Commissioner of the Bureau of Labor Statistics, are clear: "The earnings of working mothers make a difference in their families' economic situation."

Does it "Pay" a Woman to Work?

Families with two incomes generally do better than families with one income. Yet over the years many people (usually men) have argued that it costs more than it's worth for a mother to work. Just look at the direct costs of working, they'll say, the transportation and clothes and lunches. Then look at the higher tax bracket caused by her working. Well, it's true that it costs money to make money and that a family with a higher income pays more in taxes. But it's odd that no one ever says it costs too much for a father to work! If you've decided that it's right for your family to have a working mother, then go to it. Remember that the heaviest expense, for child care, will diminish as your children grow. Meanwhile, you'll be advancing on the job, earning raises and promotions, so that working will be ever-more-worthwhile.

Working Issues

Returning to the work force with small children at home forces a confrontation with specific issues, among them parental leave, child care, pay equity, and comparable worth. The external issues—those forced by institutionalized policies and attitudes—deserve considerable attention and will be discussed in a moment. But what about the internal, within-the-family issues? If you and your spouse disagree about whether it's worthwhile for a mother to work, about taking time off from the work force, or about who is responsible for child care, you may have an ongoing argument on your hands. That argument can be extremely divisive. I recall meeting a young couple in a New Hampshire campground, where

the father stayed each day with their 3-year-old daughter
while the mother drove to work in a nearby town. We
chatted, as campground acquaintances do, and learned
that the couple had been married before—to each other.
"I didn't want her to work after Debbie was born," Al
said, "and she wouldn't quit her job. So we divorced.
But then we decided we really wanted to make it work,
so we got married again."

Our New Hampshire meeting was two decades ago,
and the scenario would be less likely (although not impossible) today. Today's young parents, both working outside the home, are more likely to argue over who will
change how many diapers and who will work how many
hours. It may not be possible to predict how you will
react once you're immersed in the situation, but take
some time, now, to weigh your feelings and try to reach
an agreement.

Parental Leave

In 1960, when I was expecting my first child, I was
required to leave my job at pregnancy's midpoint; four
and a half months, my employer believed, was as far as
a pregnant woman could go. In 1985 an unmarried sci-
ence teacher in a Long Island school district fought, and
won, the right to stay on the job till her child was born.
In 1960 I never discussed maternity leave or my right
to return to the job; I assumed, along with my employer,
that I would stay at home and tend to my child. In 1985,
women can and do return to their jobs after leaves of
varying duration.

I started my family, from this point of view, a few
years too soon. Title VII of the Civil Rights Act of 1964
as amended in 1978 specifically prohibits discrimination
because of pregnancy. Employers cannot refuse to employ
a woman because of pregnancy or terminate her, force
her to go on leave at an arbitrary point during pregnancy,
or penalize her because of pregnancy in reinstatement
rights—including credit for previous service, accrued

retirement benefits, and accumulated seniority. Employers may not legally deny to pregnant employees the same benefits they extend to sick employees.

But current law (unlike the law in seventy-five other countries) does not require an employer to provide a specific number of weeks for maternity leave, to permit paternity leave, or to pay for leave time for either parent. Some major corporations have led the way in providing leave time, but this leave is usually restricted to mothers, is rarely more than six weeks in duration, and is often unpaid. In November 1985 a blue-ribbon panel organized by the Yale Bush Center in Child Development and Social Policy made sweeping recommendations for a national policy on infant care. It includes mandatory availability of leaves of at least six months for childbirth and infant care, with partial income replacement—at least 75 percent of salary—for at least three months, continuation of employee benefits, and guaranteed job security for the entire six-month period. The proposal would apply to both mothers and fathers.

This sweeping recommendation may face rough going since a more modest congressional proposal has yet to be adopted. The Parental and Medical Leave Act of 1986, introduced in March 1986, would require up to eighteen weeks leave for parents (mother *or* father) who choose to stay home with a newborn, newly adopted, or seriously ill child, and six months' leave for pregnancy-related and other temporary disabilities. (There's an argument, of course, that pregnancy is not a disability.) There is no provision for pay in this measure (the requirement is for unpaid leave), although seniority and pension rights would be retained. The bill also provides for a commission to study and make recommendations within two years for a national paid parental and disability leave policy. The idea of guaranteed unpaid leave is wildly controversial, it seems, so that movement toward paid leave must take place very slowly.

Where does this leave you? If you work for an enlightened employer you may be able to take two or three

months in unpaid leave, before and after the birth, before
you return to work. Don't have an uncomfortable pregnancy or guess wrong on your due date, however, or
you'll wind up with most of your leave time before birth
instead of after. If you work for a *very* enlightened
employer, part or all of your leave time may be paid.
And, in a very few instances, you may actually find an
employer permitting paternity leave. Since more and
more young fathers today are taking an active interest
in their children and an active role in child care—25
percent of new fathers, according to one recent study,
expect to be the primary care-giver to their babies when
their wives first return to work—this may be the wave
of the future.

Child Care

When mother or father returns to work, someone has
to care for the baby. Who will that someone be? "We've
been through three housekeepers, and Jacob is only two,"
says Alyse, who returned to her full-time advertising job
shortly after Jacob's birth. "It's nerve-wracking, but it
would be more nerve-wracking for me to stay at home."

A full-time housekeeper is one child care option, probably the most expensive option. There are many others,
both in homes (your own or others) and group centers.
Sally Wendkos Olds, in *The Working Parents Survival
Guide*, says that children under 3 are most often cared
for individually in their own or other people's homes,
children between 3 and 6 are most often cared for in
family day care (paid care, usually of several children,
by a nonrelative) or in the home of a family member.
Children over the age of 6 spend about six hours a day
in school but are watched by neighbors, relatives, or
babysitters in the before- and after-school hours. With
all the controversy surrounding group day care centers,
they accommodate relatively few young children, only
19 percent in mid-1982. Most are cared for in home
settings.

Many parents use an ad hoc "mix and match" system
of child care, which creates great strain. It's hard to
concentrate on your work if you're uncertain of your child
care arrangements. It's hard to get along well with your
spouse, if only one of you bears the burden for making
those arrangements. One parent explains her situation:
"We have a babysitter, but she has a child of her own.
If her youngster is sick, and this last winter she's been
sick a lot, I have to call my aunt to come in. If my aunt
isn't available, I have to stay home; my husband can
never take the time. It's so hard to find a good babysitter
that I don't want to let her go, but I may have to."

Sometimes parents take turns, reducing child care costs
but increasing exhaustion levels. Sheila works the mid-
night-to-8 a.m. shift as a registered nurse, while Dave
works 9 to 5; she naps while the baby naps, and, so far,
it's working out. There may be problems later, when the
baby outgrows naps and Sheila can't sleep during the
day. And there are problems of another sort now, because
Sheila and Dave seldom see one another and because,
when either has a day off, household chores are stacked
up and waiting. "We're both earning decent incomes,"
Sheila complains, "but all we do is work at our jobs and
work at home."

Some children are left to fend for themselves. This is
not an option when you've just had a baby, but some
children over the age of 10 or so thrive on independence.
Just be sure you and your spouse agree that this is the
right course; "Alan thinks I'm a terrible mother because
I let Kim come home to an empty house; we fight about
it constantly. But Kim doesn't like babyitters, and I think
he's mature." And just be sure, if you give your child a
key, that you've established enforceable ground rules for
behavior, that you check frequently by telephone, and
that you have emergency back-up care nearby.

When it comes to paying for child care, some odd
attitudes prevail, attitudes which remind me of the arguments that it doesn't "pay" for a woman to work. Rutgers
University social scientist Lionel Tiger described a fed-

eral judge of his acquaintance, a woman with two children, in a *Vogue* round-table discussion: "Out of her salary, which I believe was $59,- or $69,000 a year, she had to pay the child care, and she had to pay for two shifts of child-carers because she worked essentially a sixteen-hour day. I pointed out to her that her husband, who was earning at least $200,000 a year, might share a part of that burden; but she felt she was responsible for those expenditures."

No mother, including this judge, works for herself alone. Whether her primary reason for working is economic necessity or the rewards of fulfillment, her working contributes to the family. It contributes economically and it contributes in terms of overall satisfaction. Why, then, should she assume that she alone must pay all the expenses of earning that income? Why should her husband expect her to do so? The children are a shared responsibility, and so is their care. Yet entrenched attitudes and social custom often add a layer of guilt to the practical complexities of being a working parent.

Government policies don't help. Child care policies in the United States, like parental leave policies, are controversial. Some people believe that official support of child care facilities encourages mothers to leave their children and go out to work, and that such encouragement undermines family life. Others recognize that many families need the financial contribution that a working mother can make, and that it should be every individual's choice whether to work inside or outside the home.

Those mothers who need to earn and those who want to earn need safe, reliable places to leave their children. Federal legislation has been introduced to support child care. Some corporations—about 1,800 in 1985, up from just 40 in 1978—have taken the lead in providing workplace child care centers and in subsidizing child care for employees, spurred on by the 1981 tax act which made these expenses deductible to the company. (Cash subsidies for child care are also not taxed as income to the employee.) Another 300 companies have referral services to help parents find day care in their own neighborhoods. But there are some six million employers in the United States, and most parents are on their own, using various child care methods at various times.

Unless you're able to manage a Sheila-and-David routine, sharing child care between parents, or are lucky enough to have a loving relative or friend who can care for your child without pay, you're likely to find child care a major drain on your budget. Studies show that child care is the fourth largest item in many families' budgets, after taxes, housing, and food. An occasional babysitter can cost a few hundred dollars a year; full-time care is far, far more. On the expensive end of the scale: A full-time in-your-home housekeeper who may cost from a low of $75 or $100 a week to well over $300 a week, plus room and board. Next most costly is the child care center with a good adult-child ratio, an educational program, and health services; such centers cost from about $50 a week to $80 or more. Family day care, where children are tended by a care-giver in her home, is the least expensive, running $20 to $50 a week. It is also the most variable, since care is usually dependent on a single unlicensed individual. Some family homes are terrific, others leave a lot to be desired. Yet over two-thirds of all children and 85 percent of infants in child care are cared for in family day care programs.

Which type of child care you'll use will depend on what you can afford as well as on what's available in your community. Very little group care is available for infants. It may take some careful searching, as well as some false starts, before you find the child care that's right for you and for your child. If possible, do some research before your child is born. But be prepared to make a change at a later date, if you think a change is warranted. And line up back-up care, particularly if you're relying on a single care-giver, in case of emergency.

The *child care tax credit* may ease the financial burden. If you pay for care for a child under the age of 15 or for a disabled dependent of any age so that you can go to work, under current federal tax law you may claim a credit ranging from $480 to $720 a year depending on your income; the amount is doubled for two or more children. The person you pay may be anyone, including a relative, as long as the relative is not also your dependent. The place may be anywhere—your home, someone else's home, a day care center or school or camp. Tuition does not qualify, but the portion of tuition that covers an after-school program may; ask the school to itemize its bills so that applicable costs will be clear. The credit is available to all eligible taxpayers, no matter how much you earn.

Pay Equity

Drive past a road crew today and you are likely to see new signs—no longer "Men at Work" but "People Working." Yet, as you return to work to cope with the expenses of child-rearing you may become increasingly aware of the gap between men's and women's wages. That gap has gotten a lot of publicity, with the famous (or infamous) 59-cent button indicating that women earn 59 cents for every dollar earned by men. In fact, that's not quite true. Over the five-year period from 1979 to 1984, according to the Bureau of Labor Statistics, the earnings ratio has fluctuated between 61 and 67 percent, with the overall trend generally upward. But the ratio varies by age. Among younger workers, those under age 25, women earned 90 percent as much as men in 1983. It varies by marital status, with single women and divorced women earning more than married women; averages are skewed here, though, by the fact that many married women work part-time, or at lower-paying jobs close to home, so that they can be available to their children. And it varies by occupation. Female teachers, lawyers, and computer programmers earn from 81 to 88 percent as much as their male colleagues, while saleswomen average about half of salesmen's earnings.

Part of the problem stems from the fact that women

have followed an in-and-out pattern of labor force participation, typically staying home for several years to raise children. Part undoubtedly stems from lingering sexism, from employers believing that male heads of families need more money or that females lack commitment to work and won't stay on the job. Out-and-out discrimination is one of the reasons for women's segregation into low-paying jobs, according to a report issued in late 1985 by the National Academy of Sciences. And part stems from the fact that women are still concentrated in jobs that have traditionally been "women's work." Almost half of all women work in occupations that are at least 80 percent female. The higher the percentage of female workers in any occupation, the National Academy of Sciences notes in its report, the less that occupation is paid. Five of the top ten occupations employing women are sales and clerical: typists, secretaries, bookkeepers, cashiers, and salesworkers. Two are professional but (because they are traditionally held by women?) low-paying: registered nurses and elementary school teachers. Two more are the service occupations of waitresses and nurses' aides.

Many women, especially younger women, are moving into higher-paying jobs. Many are becoming lawyers and managers and computer programmers. Many are moving into jobs traditionally held by men—telephone installers, construction workers, engineers. Many are planning to stay in the work force, even after having children, which will add to seniority and hence to income. But most are still, and will probably remain, in jobs at the lower end of the pay scale.

The concentration of women in "women's jobs" has led to the expansion of the widely supported concept of pay equity (equal pay for equal work) to the far more controversial notion of comparable worth (equal pay for comparable jobs). How to determine what jobs are comparable? In some instances it's easy. Oregon prison matrons earned $200 a month less than deputy sheriffs; both guarded prisoners. In other cases it's not so easy. Are

librarians "worth" the same pay as air-conditioning con-
tractors? How do you decide? One way to decide is via
an evaluation committee, such as the one established by
Washington State in one of the first comparable-worth
cases; that committee rated jobs and set salaries by using
a point system, with points awarded for knowledge and
skills, mental demands, accountability, and working conditions. In Washington State, the study revealed that the
jobs held primarily by women were generally paid 20 to
30 percent less than jobs that earned the same number
of points but were generally filled by men. National statistics back up the Washington findings: The more a job
category is dominated by women, the less it pays—with
the compensation going down about $42 a year for each
additional percentage point of women employed in the
category.

Studies and statistics notwithstanding, comparable worth
is controversial. Proponents say that it's no more radical
a notion than desegregation of schools was in the 1950s
and that it is a cause which is right and just. Opponents
say that wage evaluations are inherently subjective and
that efforts to enforce comparable worth will lead inevitably to federal bureaucracy and federal control. Either
way, because it runs counter to businesses' entrenched
right to set salaries according to market forces, comparable worth may be as slow in coming to this nation as
the metric system.

Meanwhile, what can you do if you suspect your pay
is unfairly low? You should know that federal law prohibits unequal pay for men and women who work in the
same place and whose jobs require equal skill, effort and
responsibility. Employers may base wage differentials
on seniority or on merit or on production, but not on
gender. If you think you are not receiving equal pay for
equal work, you may file a complaint with the Equal
Employment Opportunity Commission, which enforces
the Equal Pay Act. If investigation reveals a violation,
the EEOC will negotiate with the employer for a settlement including back pay and appropriate raises in pay

scales to correct the violation of the law. You may also sue privately. Filing a complaint or filing suit is not done lightly—it won't endear you to your employer, or make your workdays very comfortable—but it may be a step you feel you must take in the interests of both equity and the income your family needs.

No Superpeople Here

You may need to work, you may want to work, yet you may find that holding down a full-time job while caring for child and house is just too much. Stories abound of women rising at 5 a.m. to dress and feed children and get them to day care, rushing off to a stress-filled job, and then back to tend to children and house at night. Stories also abound of women, collapsing under the weight of stress-filled days, rebelling against this Superwoman syndrome. Some rebel by refusing to do it all, by insisting that husbands share the work of children and house. Others rebel by reducing the outside work load while not giving up income-producing work altogether. Some decide that the marriage itself no longer works.

Ideally, men should realize that their children and their homes are as much their jobs as their wives'. Practically, although more and more men are pitching in and some are assuming the major role, sometimes changing jobs to make time available, the primary responsibility in most families still rests with women. As the first issue of *Ms.* magazine put it, the click of recognition can occur when your family is rushing around being supportive so that you can work—but you're still the one who has to remember to get the lamb chops they're willing to cook. Even where women earn more than men—and 12 percent of American women earn more than the men in their lives—remembering the lamb chops falls to them.

Many women, therefore, try to ease the burden by cutting back on work outside the home. A lucky few find their employers willing to reduce work hours, to schedule a four-day week, for example, instead of five. Some high-level professional/executive women will settle for working a five-day forty-hour week instead of six days and seventy to eighty hours; an example is an attorney who chose to work for the government instead of in a highly charged private practice. Some look to full-time jobs closer to home; "I'm still a full-charge bookkeeper, but in the suburbs near home instead of in the city; if the baby gets sick, I'm nearby, and when she's well I've still cut down my commuting time."

Some women find shared-time jobs, where a single full-time job is split betwen two workers. Often these are clerical office jobs but sometimes they are at higher levels. One group of physicians, described in the Langer Report, arranged a three-day-a-week hospital schedule so that each could be home more often with her own children. Many women opt for part-time jobs, keeping a hand in the work force while putting career advancement on hold until the children are older. And a growing number create their own jobs, finding remunerative work that they can do in their own homes and on their own time schedule. Among the job titles of these self-employed women: jewelry maker, typist, personnel consultant.

All of this may sound rosier than it actually is. If you've worked long and hard to advance in your career, you may now find yourself marking time, if not actually slipping backward, because your attention is focused elsewhere. If you depend on your full-time salary, you may not have the luxury of cutting back. Even if you can afford to work fewer hours, you may not readily find an employer willing to indulge your fancy or a self-made job that will be financially rewarding. Many helpful books on the market deal with job-seeking; I won't attempt to duplicate their information here. But I will emphasize yet again the importance of communicating with your spouse. Define your mutual goals and the way in which you will work, together, to meet those goals. If it will take two incomes to get where you want to go, then work out, together, how you will regard both incomes and how you will divide the household child care responsibilities to make both incomes possible.

Children and Money

One of the tasks that goes with parenthood, even as you struggle with the costs of child-rearing and your other financial concerns, is teaching your children to manage money well. The subject belongs in a chapter on new parents, because children start to pick up attitudes about money very early, long before you set out consciously to teach. Your children will realize at a very early age that money can be used to buy goods and services. They will see what you do with money, hear what you say, and pick up any differences between you and your spouse.

Those differences may be a source of tension. Initially it may be a question of how much it's necessary to spend on children—once again, a question of secondhand baby furniture versus top-of-the-line new models. Many parents, especially older parents, are electing to buy the best. Marketers are delighted with this generation of "gourmet babies," infants showered with luxury clothing, expensive toys, and classes of all description—yes, there are swimming lessons and gymnastics classes for 4-month-old babies. And advertisers are playing on the guilt feelings of working parents to sell a range of products from convenience foods to office automation. Office automation? Yes. Xerox recently ran an ad showing how Dad made it home for Sarah's birthday party, thanks to the efficiency of Xerox equipment.

Later it becomes a question of how much money to let children spend on themselves. You and your spouse, with different temperaments and different backgrounds of your own, may have conflicting thoughts on both issues. Conflict can be parent-to-parent: "At her age, all she needs are stretch suits and overalls; why must you buy velvet dresses?" And, a bit later, conflict may be on the parent-child frontier: "No, you may not buy a robot and I don't care if Donny has one." The conflict may involve grandparents: "We keep asking our folks not to bring presents to the children every time they come—the kids are at the point where they ask for the presents before they say hello—but it doesn't do any good."

You and your spouse may find yourselves thoroughly at odds over spending. "My husband didn't have much as a child and he wants our children to have everything. I think they're going to be spoiled brats." You may also be at odds over the question of giving children an allowance. Those who are opposed offer a variety of arguments: "Nothing in this world is free, and children, like adults, should work for what they get. I'll pay little ones for chores around the house, but as soon as they're old enough I expect the kids to get outside jobs and earn their own spending money." Or, as another parent puts it: "The children have everything they could possibly need—music lessons, sports equipment, clothing. If we don't buy something, the grandparents do. What would they do with spending money?" Some parents simply want to retain control. "My husband wants to screen every request for money so that he'll know what the kids are doing. If we just 'give' them money, he says, they can do as they please."

Parents who favor allowances (as I do) muster many arguments as well. "When we give Beth an allowance," a mother from Michigan points out, "it becomes Beth's responsibility to make the money last for the week. She has to realize that if she spends it on one thing, then she won't have it to spend on another. She can't come to us for more. What's more, we know how much she's spending. Before we started the allowance, when she came to us every time something came up, the outlay varied enormously." When you don't give an allowance, moreover, you encourage chiildren to be manipulative, to "get Mommy (or Daddy) in a good mood" before requesting money. When you don't give an allowance, you may be encouraging your children to play one parent off against the other. An allowance, in my opinion, is the single best way to teach children to manage money objectively, to reduce the emotional byplay that surrounds money in much of our lives.

If you choose to give an allowance, do keep it objective: Determine the amount, in consultation with the child, and then be consistent. Give the allowance on a regular basis, so that the children know what they are getting and when and can plan accordingly. Decide what the allowance must cover (Scout dues, for example, or lunch money) and then be sure to include a discretionary sum as well, a no-strings-attached amount that is the real decision-making tool. Be realistic, in terms of what things cost these days; there are no more 10¢ candy bars or comic books. Giving too much money is bad, because a child won't learn to set priorities and make decisions. Giving too little is also bad, because the allowance is then simply a source of frustration. Review the allowance regularly, every couple of months with small children and once a year with older ones, to be sure the amount is still appropriate. And, because the allowance is a learning tool, keep it independent of the way your children behave or the chores they are asked to perform. If you attach monetary value to behavior, fining a child a quarter because he's rude to Aunt Molly, you're providing an easy route to atonement for misbehavior. If you pay children for routine household chores, you're making money too important. Your children should do chores because they're members of the family. They won't always be eager to do them, whether they are paid or not, and it's better to keep money out of the equation.

If you choose *not* to give an allowance, you can still give your children objective lessons in money management. Try to be consistent as you respond to their requests for money. If you can objectively decide on the merits of a request regardless of how rushed you are or the mood you are in (which many parents find takes the wisdom of Solomon and the patience of a saint!), then you will avoid some of the unhealthy psychological patterns that can go hand in hand with tight parental control. And, if you are consistent, the children will learn to make reasonable requests, backed by information, rather than relying solely on techniques of persuasion. Try to be flexible, too, so that control doesn't breed rebellion. Children, like adults, occasionally need to spend money foolishly; they may "need" one more record album just as you "need" one more pair of shoes or household gadget. The purchases we make, children and adults alike, fulfill psychological needs as well as practical ones.

Even if you don't give an allowance, you may still decide to let the children spend some of the money you would otherwise spend on their behalf: for lunch money, for example, or bus fare or sheet music for their lessons. Try to give them some decision-making as well as spending authority—even if it's deciding to skip dessert in favor of a comic book—so that they learn about handling money beyond the pleasure that spending brings. And keep track of just how much you're doling out on request. You don't have to give a regular allowance in order to set reasonable limits on spending.

It's easy enough to outline the arguments for and against allowances and to make up your mind what to do. But what happens if you and your spouse reach opposite conclusions? The partner with more power (because he or she earns the larger income?) may win the dispute. If this happens, the loser may add the issue to a long mental list of slights generated by power . . . and the children may pick up the message that one parent dominates the other and that money is an instrument of domination. It would be better, by far, to talk through your differences and reach consensus.

Legal Obligations

As a matter of law, parents must provide reasonable and proper support for their children. As a matter of fact, what is reasonable and proper varies according to family circumstances; in some states, well-to-do parents are considered responsible for college and postgraduate education, a responsibility that extends parental responsibility well beyond the years of childhood. On the other hand, parents are ordinarily not responsible for their children's debts. Some states, however, have passed legislation making parents liable for damages caused by children and for debts incurred by children. The law aside, such responsibility may be a source of disagreement between wife and husband. "He ordered those magazines; let him pay for them," says one father about a 16-year-old whose mother is willing to bail him out.

You also, contrary to what many people think, have no direct legal control over your children's money. "If your child earns or inherits money or receives money in the form of support payments," says the American Bar Association in its useful booklet, "Law & Marriage: Your Legal Guide," "this money must be used for the child's benefit. Officially (unless a court appoints someone else), you are the *guardian* of your child's money and can be held legally responsible for managing it properly and using it on the child's behalf." Uncle John's bequest to namesake Johnny may be invested toward Johnny's college education or used to send Johnny to summer camp; you shouldn't use it to redecorate the family room.

The College Crunch

Planning ahead for changing financial circumstances makes it a lot easier to have a baby in the first place. And planning ahead for college can make college costs manageable. Those costs are enormous. In the 1985–86 school year, the average cost for one year at a four-year public college for a resident student was $5,314; at a four-year private college the average was $9,659. At Harvard (the fifth most expensive college on the College Board's list) the 1985–86 year cost about $17,210. Assume inflation at a rate of 6 percent (modest in terms of recent inflation rates) and the figure will come close to doubling in ten short years.

If you want to send your children to college, you should start planning now. Your biggest current purchase may be disposable diapers, but hard as it may be to believe, college will be here before you know it. There may well be loans and grants and the student's own earnings to ease the burden when the freshman beanie is donned, but you can still figure on a major outlay out of your own pocket. With one child, and an annual income of $45,000, financial aid officers expect parents to contribute at least $6,570 toward the cost of a year at college. That's after-tax dollars. That outlay will be easier to manage if it comes out of accumulated savings rather than out of current income.

Disciplined saving can build your college fund through compounding interest. It's also been possible, until recently, to reduce taxes on savings and let college funds build still faster by putting savings into a child's name. Both custodial accounts under the Uniform Gift to Minors Act and special forms of trusts, most notably the so-called Clifford trust, have been widely used to "share income" among family members. By making gifts to children of cash or securities, parents could have the resulting interest or dividend taxed at the child's low or nonexistent federal income tax rate. There were drawbacks to such income-sharing, especially the fact that money given remained given. A child could choose to run off with a motorcycle gang once he or she reached legal age, and the money could go along. There was also the argument that less financial aid is usually forthcoming when a prospective student has sizable assets. The issue may now be moot, since legislation in the federal hopper in spring 1986, as this is written, short-circuits this route to college saving. Under the proposed legislation, custodial accounts or Clifford trusts set up by parents for children under the age of 14 will be taxed at the parent's tax rate. Once a child is over 14, his or her own tax rate will apply. But funds given by other people to a child of any age will still be taxed at the child's rate. If your parents want to set up a trust for your children's college education, there-

fore, interest on the trust funds will be taxed at the child's
rate. Just be careful about passing money to your parents
for them to use in setting up a trust; the IRS will probably
scrutinize such transactions very carefully.

Whatever legislation actually passes (and you can expect
tax law to change between the time your child is born
and the time college approaches), whatever savings method
you choose, you may find yourself wondering just how
much you should contribute toward your child's college
education in the first place. Some parents believe that
college means much more to the child who earns it. "I'll
give Jeff a place to live, if he wants to go to college while
living at home," one father says. "But he'll have to pay
the tuition himself." Others want to provide everything,
including a college education, to get their children off
to the best possible start. Sort out your own feelings,
and try to agree on a course of action, because you will
find yourself facing some specific questions as your children grow: When Jill starts to earn money from a part-
time job at the dry cleaners will she be required to save
her earnings toward college? Or allowed to spend them
on the ski trips she desperately wants? Will you tell Kim
to take out his own college loans? Or will you go into
debt on his behalf? Do you think that borrowing for
college is okay, without regard to who does the borrowing? Or do you firmly believe that the money ought to
be saved in advance?

With escalating college costs (escalating more rapidly,
in recent years, than the pace of inflation) it's extremely
difficult if not impossible for students to work their own
way through college. Students who do carry a heavy work
load either extend the college years or find themselves
with scant time for their studies and no time for social
life. Most parents who are able to do so, therefore, lend
a helping hand. At one end of the helping spectrum are
the parents who will pay the full costs of tuition, room,
board, and books but who ask their children to shoulder
the couple of thousand dollars a year it takes for transportation and social life (that beer and pizza is expensive).

At the other end, out of economic necessity or philosophic belief, are the parents who will provide a specified fraction of college costs, or a specified dollar amount, and have the children do the rest. Try to sort out how you feel, and how your spouse feels, before your youngsters get anywhere near the college years.

The Long Run

It's hard to picture, as the euphoric (and exhausted) parent of a newborn, but children grow up very quickly. During their growing-up years, you have a lot to consider. You have legal responsibilities to your children, and you have your own self-imposed responsibilities. Here are some of the things you may want to consider.

Insurance

It's amazing how word gets around when a baby is born. Some of the first people to know the good news seem to be life insurance salespeople. But don't automatically shut your ears just because it's a salesperson calling. Life insurance, on both parents, may be a very good idea indeed when there is financial responsibility for a child. A two-income couple should own enough life insurance on each parent to alleviate the financial burden survivors will face in doing without that income. A one-income couple should consider the costs of replacing the care-giver's services and should probably also consider insurance on each partner. This means that you should try to determine how much your survivors will need over the years until the children are grown, calculate their income from other sources—including on-the-job life insurance, Social Security benefits, and other assets—and then buy as much life insurance as you can afford to make up the gap. This generally means buying *term insurance* which, because it is pure insurance with no built-in cash value and no loan provisions, provides more insurance for less money for most people under the age of 50. Term insurance will increase in cost either every year or every five years, depending on the type of policy you buy; it is usually guaranteed renewable up to age 65 or 70 and convertible, without a medical exam, to permanent insurance.

Permanent insurance is more expensive when bought by younger people, but its premium is fixed for life. Permanent insurance, also called whole life or ordinary insurance, also has accumulating cash value (regarded by some as a form of forced savings) against which you may borrow. Other forms of life insurance, such as *universal* or *variable* insurance, include flexible premiums and investment-oriented yields. A life insurance trust, using one of the permanent forms of insurance, can be designed to provide enough money to raise a child plus enough for college. Talk to a competent and reliable insurance agent in determining the best way to meet your family's insurance needs.

And don't overlook *disability income* insurance. This is a form of insurance that will replace lost income if you are injured or ill. You may have some disability income insurance through your job or by way of Social Security; if not, or if it is inadequate, consider buying an individual policy. Look for a policy that provides benefits if you can't work at your customary occupation; under some policies you can be denied benefits if you can do anything at all, including stuffing envelopes at home. And look at one that does not require total in-hospital or at-home confinement; you may be disabled and still want some fresh air. Buy a policy that covers both accident and illness, and keep premium costs down by electing a waiting period of at least ninety days before benefits start. You shouldn't need insurance the first week or month you're laid up, and you should have enough of a savings cushion to cover three months. Disability income insurance is designed to replace lost income, but a couple of companies now write policies on homemakers; while expensive, such a policy might be worth considering if you have small children and would find the cost of child care and homemaking services prohibitive if you were laid up for an extended period.

Writing a Will

"If anything happens to me, my wife (or husband) will get everything anyway," many people say, "so I don't need to write a will." It ain't, in the words of the song, necessarily so. If you die intestate, without a will, most states will distribute your assets among your spouse and children. But there are a couple of things you should know: (1) The distribution may not be according to your wishes; it may even be in a way that will leave your survivor strapped for funds. Your survivor might receive half of your estate, for example, with your children sharing the other half. If the children are minors, your survivor may not be able to spend their money on their behalf without court appproval. (2) Your surviving spouse will not automatically be the legal guardian of minor children, if you don't designate him or her as guardian in a will. Usually, of course, a surviving parent is named guardian. But court expenses will be involved, even if the surviving parent is the children's natural parent. If he or she is an adoptive or stepparent, there may be a challenge to the guardianship. Protect your spouse, and your children, by naming a guardian in your will.

You and your spouse should each have a will. The simplest form, if you're of like minds, is to leave everything to each other (thereby qualifying for a total exclusion from federal estate taxes on the estate of the first to die) and then to the children. You should each name a guardian for the children. If assets are extensive, you might want to name both a guardian of the person, to raise the children, and a guardian of the property, to manage the money. It's most important to select a kindred spirit to raise your children, but that warm and loving person who shares your values may not have the best money sense. In this case, even with more modest assets, you can split the burden by naming two guardians.

Both of you need wills, incidentally, even if only one of you is currently earning an income. All kinds of legal complications can otherwise arise. In one instance, a young couple died in an auto accident. He had a will, she did not. He died first, by a few minutes, so that she inherited everything. Then, because she didn't have a will, the courts had to step in and arrange both for distribution of assets and guardianship of the children. The grandparents disagreed, and the children were subjected to much unnecessary unpleasantness.

While your children are young, you may want to leave money for them (after the death of your spouse) in trust so that it will be managed in their behalf. Where considerable sums are at stake, many people structure their estates so that funds are distributed incrementally as children reach the ages of 25, 30, and even 35. You and your spouse should discuss what you think is best for your children and then review your wills periodically to see if revision is needed. Just be sure that you make your wills in the first place. Too many people procrastinate, reluctant to face the thought of death, and die without having made wills. What those people are actually doing is dying without making provision for their families. And *that* is irresponsible.

Money Traps for Parents

• Your lifestyle, and your relationship, will change with the birth of your first child. Be prepared for a shift in the balance of power as well if one income is suspended, even temporarily. Before this happens, talk through just how you will handle the remaining income to preserve autonomy for you both.

• Underestimating the costs of child-rearing can put a great strain on your marriage. Disagreeing about how much or how little to spend on your children can do so as well.

• While pay equity and comparable worth are socio-economic issues that must be addressed in the outside world, you and your spouse should consider your own attitudes toward work for pay and work inside the home. Both partners, whatever their relative income levels, deserve respect. Both partners should work out, together, responsibility for household maintenance and child care.

• Using money to reward or punish children sets the stage for money problems in their later lives. Try, instead, to treat money objectively, giving your children an allowance so they will learn to manage money well.

·8·

Mid-Life Matters

YOU'VE WEATHERED the early years, you've reared the children, and now you're on the threshold of a whole new experience. A century ago, this was the end of life or, at the very least, it held no surprises. Today it is both the beginning of a new life stage and a time of redefined expectations.

The new life stage results from a combination of lengthened life expectancy and smaller families. The average life expectancy at birth today is 70.3 for men, 77.9 for women. If there are only two children, born by the time parents are in their mid-thirties, the second child should become independent when parents are in their mid-fifties; this is a decade later than it would be if today's young couples were having babies in their twenties, but it still leaves parents with fifteen years or more of an empty nest.

Redefined expectations take place partly because of this lengthy empty-nest period; husband-wife relationships, which may previously have centered on the children, must now be refocused if the marriage is to thrive. Redefined expectations also take place because people expect more out of life. A man may decide to make a mid-life career change. A woman may do the same, although her change may be from full-time homemaker to paid employee.

At the same time, many issues confront the mid-life couple. Income may be leveling off, as earning power peaks—unless a second income is added, which may add tensions of its own. Men may be ready to coast a bit, after years of striving, only to find their wives eager to demonstrate their own abilities to the outside world. Children may be grown, yet still in need of financial and emotional support, just as parents are aging and beginning to need help. In this chapter we'll examine the ramifications of all of these issues, and what you can do to cope.

When Wives Return to Work

Although more and more mothers are returning to the work force either shortly after their children are born or by the time those children enter first grade, many women continue as full-time homemakers until the children leave home. Then, whether because of the pressure of college costs or because of the quiet of an empty house, many elect to seek outside work. When they do, there is a resounding impact on the marriage.

Sometimes the marriage doesn't last. Nancy, an accomplished artist, took a job as a high school art teacher when the youngest of her three children reached tenth grade. "She was never there for me after she started working. We didn't need the money," her now ex-husband complains, "and I didn't think she should work." Whether it was really Nancy's job that led to the divorce, or whether there was underlying discontent, the job was certainly the catalyst. With her enthusiasm about her work, she had less time and energy to devote to her husband's well-being . . . and he didn't see why his comfort should be disrupted for the sake of her job.

Sometimes a marriage is strengthened. "I was completely boring once the children grew up, with nothing at all to talk about. It's a wonder John put up with me. But I finally took his not-so-subtle hints to get out and *do* something, and we're getting along much better. We've taken a hard look at our goals and our priorities, and it's made us both much happier."

Even when a mid-life marriage is strengthened by a wife's return to the work force, there are some adjustments to make along the way. It will probably be different for today's young couples, entering marriage with the expectation that both husband and wife will work at paying jobs, that both husband and wife will share in running the household. But if you're now in your forties or fifties, you were brought up with different expectations, and you've probably lived much of your married life by different rules. Under those rules the husband is usually the breadwinner, providing financial support for the family; the wife is usually the homemaker, literally making a home and providing emotional warmth and support. When she enters the work force, a number of things happen: She becomes independent by earning money of her own and insists on sharing in decision-making; she has less time to maintain the home and wants help from her husband; she has less energy to provide emotional support to her husband and she may need such support herself. All of these things may constitute a threat to her husband and, therefore, to the marriage.

The threat manifests itself in different ways to different people. For some, particularly where the wife works out of economic necessity, the husband may feel less of a man because he is unable to support his family. Such men often salve their egos by pigeonholing their wives' incomes: "It's just till we put the kids through college." For others, the relatively affluent whose wives work for emotional rewards rather than economic ones, the husband may simply feel, like Nancy's husband, that she is no longer "there." "While homebound wives have traditionally depended on their husbands' achievements for much of their sense of worth," social psychologist Zick Rubin wrote in *Psychology Today*, "husbands have been at least as dependent on their wives—as listeners, consolers, and ego-builders—for their emotional sustenance. When the wife has a career of her own, however, the exchange is altered." Now *she* may be asking *him* to review her presentation to a client, instead of finding time to comment on his work. Now *she* may be late getting home, and ask *him* to start preparing dinner.

When both partners need support and no one has time to provide support, the emotional balance shifts.

The balance of power shifts when a wife begins to earn, even when both partners support her move. Suddenly she has money of her own to spend. She may have had a generous "allowance" in the past, she may even have handled his income and the family budget, but money of her own makes a difference. "He earned the money, so he decided how to spend it. Sure, I handled it but all that meant was balancing the checkbook and writing the checks. When it came to deciding where to go on vacation, or even which house to buy, the decisions were all his. Now I have my own bank account and my own money to spend, so I can make my own decisions."

Some husbands react to the threat of their wives' independent decision-making—even when, on the surface, they supported her return to work—by undermining her efforts. They may sabotage her job: "I've suddenly realized that Jay picks a fight, like clockwork, the night before I have to make a presentation to a client," notes an account executive with an advertising agency. "It took me a while to put two and two together—sometimes the arguments were so silly that I didn't know what we were fighting about—but now that I see the pattern, I'm beginning to understand." And they may refuse to share the burden in the home, in the familiar scenario of "I don't mind if she works as long as my dinner is on the table at six o'clock." As psychologist Morton H. Shaevitz put it in *The Superwoman Syndrome* (written by his wife, Marjorie Hansen Shaevitz), "Men would like to have some things different and keep others the same. They would like to have the financial burden shared and their personal lives run smoothly. . . . Most men are quite happy to have their wives work—as long as that work does not interfere with the ongoing nature of the relationship."

In truth, when husband and wife both hold paying jobs, dinner is seldom on the table at six o'clock. And the dishes, the laundry, vacuuming carpets, and scrubbing toilet bowls may have to be either farmed out to paying help, if this is possible, or shared by both partners. Otherwise, if one must do it all, she will suffer— and so will the marriage, because an overtired, overstressed wife is not very good company.

Some wives remain in marriages with husbands who are resistant to change. As one woman wrote to *Good Housekeeping* magazine, "During my fourteen years of marriage I have held a full-time job and earned my Ph. D. at night. Through it all my husband refused to lift one finger to help out around the house. Together we now earn more than $100,000 a year (I earn more than half), but he will not allow me to hire any help. I spend my weekends cleaning, doing laundry, cooking, and balancing our checkbook—while he sits and does nothing!" Many women, discerning no particular rewards in such a one-sided relationship, want out.

It takes some talking through, and mutual support, if the shifting balance of power is to be taken in stride so that the needs of both partners can be met. As Francine Klagsbrun puts it in *Married People: Staying Together in the Age of Divorce*, "What struck me about the couples in first or second marriages who manage to keep their unions strong in spite of economic power pulls was the kind of step-by-step adjustment each partner made in the new circumstance of a wife working or seeking a career. Each gave the other time to get used to a way of living that undid what had come before. And in spite of angers and arguments, each seemed willing to wait it out while the other caught up." It's a "renegotiation of the underlying contract," Klagsbrun says, that can take place as long as there is mutual forbearance.

Even more forbearance may be required when the career paths of husband and wife diverge. He may be just about ready to sit back and relax, spending more time at home, just when she is ready to set loose and fly into the outer world. "I thought it was terrific when Gwen got a job with an insurance company six years ago, when she was forty-seven," a Minnesota husband says.

"I thought it was even more terrific when she got a promotion, even though it involved long hours and some out-of-town trips. But I'm fifty-eight now, and I'd like to take life a little easier. In fact, I think I'd like to retire early, so that we can do the traveling we always wanted to do. The trouble is, I'm afraid Gwen won't like the idea." Gwen *won't* like the idea. She knows what's on Fred's mind, but she doesn't yet know how to resolve the inevitable conflict. "I waited a long time to get a job like this. Now that I'm finally getting somewhere, I don't want to give it up. Yet we *did* want to travel together, and it doesn't seem fair to Fred. But I've got to be fair to me too."

More and more mid-life couples face a similar problem, the result of both shifting sociological norms as women take their place in the work force and of moderating gender differences, the gradual mellowing of men in the second half of life and the increasing independence of women. As Gail Sheehy notes in *Pathfinders*, "The average man has spent half his life building his career. Having pushed himself for twenty or thirty years along a narrow career track, he suddenly may look up and say, 'Wait a minute, when is it my time to play?' " But this husband, thinking longingly of travel or of improving his golf game or of just generally taking life easier, may have a wife, like Gwen, who is just coming into her own. "Released at least from daily responsibility for her children, she may well be looking for something in life besides another person to mother. If she plans to retool her skills with the aim of finding well-paid and satisfying work, she will not be free to be folded up like a leisure suit and taken along on pleasure trips whenever her husband has the time."

The resulting conflicts show up in many ways. Sometimes they are overtly related to the job, as in the instances of sabotage described above. Sometimes they surface in more subtle ways. Now that Marge has earned money of her own, as an instance, she and Irwin seem to be striving to outdo each other in spending. He buys a camera, she buys a watercolor painting; he outfits a full-scale basement workshop, she remodels the kitchen. There's almost a sibling rivalry at work here, as each tries to better the other.

Yet women with earned income of their own can contribute a great deal to their marriages. Many men realize, once they adjust, that they are better off both financially and emotionally in a two-income family. "I know now that she is staying with me out of choice rather than because she couldn't make a better deal," the husband of an urban planner told *The Wall Street Journal*, then adds, "Here I am pulling the responsibility wagon through life, and it's nice to know there is another strong horse beside you."

Repeated studies have shown that married women who are employed outside the home have more self-esteem than their stay-at-home counterparts. Their mid-life husbands, at least initially, may suffer from lowered self-esteem. These are, after all, men for whom a lifetime of identity has been built around being the breadwinner. But, notes Rubin, once men adjust to the idea of their wives working they begin to feel better about themselves if those wives are bringing in a respectable income. They then can point with pride, and view the wife's accomplishments as reflected glory—an ironic comment for a generation in which women so often could shine only in the reflected glory of men. But pride goes only so far. In many couples, if the wife begins to out-earn the husband, conflict surfaces once again.

When a Wife Earns More Than Her Husband

Anything that counters prevailing social norms stirs anxiety. And little goes as counter to American myth as the woman who earns more than her husband. Yet fully 6 million women, representing 12 percent of American couples, do earn more than their husbands.

The reasons vary. According to the Census Bureau,

which compiled the figures, the six million are made up
of underachieving husbands and superachieving wives.
The two may have a reciprocal relationship because, says
the bureau, "a superachieving wife may very well have
demoralizing effects on a husband, and an underachieving husband may quite possibly provide the incentive
for a wife to enter the labor force and discover talents
she otherwise would not have discovered." In fact, two
million of the women are the sole providers for their
families; their husbands are either students, ill, or unemployed. The laid-off thousands in the auto and steel
industries fit this pattern, along with managers ousted
in a merger and medical students being put through
school. These men can hardly be lumped together as
underachievers. But their wives, working part-time or
full-time, at blue-collar jobs or in professions, provide
the family income.

Others are part of two-earner couples in which the
husband earns less because he has consciously elected
an unpressured life, because his chosen field doesn't pay
well, or because his wife is in fact more motivated to
succeed. There's the couple, profiled by U.S. News &
World Report, in which a laid-back husband deliberately
steers clear of "wheeler-dealer type jobs" and content-
edly earns $16,000 a year with an electrical firm while
his wife, who admits that her "ego needs more feeding,"
earns $48,000 a year as the manager of investor com-
munications for a computer manufacturer. There's an
architect, well respected in a traditionally ill-paying
profession, married to a topflight corporate lawyer with
a six-figure income. And there's an editor whose wife is
a television reporter. All three of these couples are among
the almost 40 percent of the couples with higher-earning
wives in which the wives make at least twice as much as
their husbands. Many, of course, make just slightly more.
And, for many couples, it's a relay race as one or the
other temporarily moves ahead.

One might expect both men and women, where the
income difference is both pronounced and permanent,

to be uncomfortable with reverse income disparity, because it implies a reversal of roles. That expectation is mirrored in the title of a November 1982 *Psychology Today* article: "Real Men Don't Earn Less Than Their Wives." The problem, it seems, is that "real men" define their manhood in terms of their ability to earn. They "measure their masculinity by the size of their paycheck." But real men don't fit a single pattern and neither do their wives. There may well be problems if the higher-earning spouse, man *or* woman, wields income as a club. There may also be problems if the marriage contains two highly ambitious strivers, one of whom is outpacing the other. And there may be problems if the high-earning partner is highly visible in the outside world, where prestige is what counts. What's often difficult to deal with, says Dr. Shaevitz, "is a wife's suddenly becoming significantly more successful than her husband financially, achieving greater status and visibility. Here the man experiences the relative disparity between them as *his failure* rather than *her success.*"

Whether there is a problem at all depends on how the individuals themselves view the situation. If neither sees a problem, there may indeed be no problem. It doesn't matter who earns what. But if the higher-earning partner feels used or if the lower-earning partner feels powerless, the marriage may be in trouble. Much also depends on how the lower-earning partner feels about what he is doing. If he is driving a cab because he can't find a job suited to his Ph.D. in economics while his wife, who started as a secretary, is moving up the managerial ladder in banking, he may feel rotten. If, on the other hand, he is building a reputation as a sculptor while his wife earns the bread, he may have a very positive sense of self-worth.

Whatever your respective jobs, however, there's no need to let an unexpected (or expected) income disparity disrupt your marriage. Try, instead, to focus on what each of you brings to the relationship. It takes far more than money, after all, to support a marriage. It takes mutual respect, emotional support, sometimes even specific skills that one can share with the other. There's the couple cited by Tessa Albert Warschaw, Ph.D., in *Working Woman*: a high-earning retailing executive married to a playwright/theater director. She helped him line up backers for a new production; he coached her on speeches she had to make and helped her overcome her timidity in front of an audience. There needn't be such a specific quid pro quo, of course; it may be quite enough to lend an ear when your spouse has a problem, to lend a shoulder when one is needed. It may be enough to balance spontaneity against deliberation, an impulsive nature against a thoughtful one.

It also helps, as always, to understand oneself and to communicate with the other. Among Dr. Warschaw's strategies for a happy relationship, from her book *Rich Is Better*:

• Pay attention to your own feelings. Do you resent, if you're a man, remarks about your wife's success? Do you feel abandoned by her dedication to her work? Ask yourself, if you're a woman, whether you keep your triumphs to yourself, fearful of your partner's response should you share them. Think about whether you're criticizing him more often.

• Try to identify the real issue, which may very well have nothing to do with dollars and cents. Is it a matter of who makes the decisions in the household? Is it a question of who is dominant and who is nurturing?

• Don't, if you're the more "successful" partner, be overelated at your success. But don't deny it either. "There is a middle ground. And that is to delight with your mate in your triumph but with the same measure of tact that you would use with a female friend. To find that level," says Warschaw, "simply picture yourself as your best friend listening to you on the subject of the raise, promotion, or award you just received. Now talk as you'd like yourself heard—with absolute pleasure but without flaunting."

• Negotiate the financial aspects of your life: Decide

whether you will have joint accounts or separate ones. If the latter, decide on a basic budget and apportion your contributions to that budget on an equitable basis. Decide who pays for which luxuries over and above that budget. If you're the one who really wants to go skiing, perhaps the ski trips should come out of your pocket. Renegotiate your finances periodically. As you become comfortable with your relative income levels, and with each other, you may decide to merge separate accounts into a joint account. "Damn the income difference," is the way one woman put it. "We're a couple, and our money is our money no matter where it comes from."

Other Job Issues

Role reversal from mismatched income is not the only issue that may confront working couples. Job transfers and relocations have plagued families for a long time, usually via the man whose job was at stake. Today, when mid-life women are on the move, they face their own transfers and relocations. Sometimes two-income couples face commuter marriages.

There are some hard choices to make when one partner in a two-income couple is offered a good job in another city. It comes down to: Reject the job, accept the job and move, accept the job and live in different cities. Some corporations are making sincere efforts to find appropriate jobs for the spouse of a transferred employee but, at times, there are no such jobs to be found. That's when the decision boils down to rejecting the transfer— and, perhaps, jeopardizing career progress—or assuming the burden of a two-city marriage.

More and more couples, although no one knows exactly how many, seem to be embarking on commuter marriages. It's a rough road to travel, and it's also an expensive road. On top of endless hours in the air or on the road, just to get to one another, there are the costs of maintaining two households plus lengthy long-distance telephone calls. And, of course, there's emotional fallout as well. Commuter couples tend to be high-earning high-achieving individuals, accustomed to putting the job first, but commuting adds what may be one strain too many to the relationship. It may, once again, be a matter of power, of a delicate shifting of the balance in the marriage, of whose career—and hence which person—comes first. Money is seldom the actual issue but it can easily become a symbol of discontent.

Stay-at-Home Wives

Not every marriage turns upside down in the middle years. Not every wife chooses to join the workaday world. Not every husband yearns to be footloose and fancy-free. Husbands may continue to be sole breadwinners, while their wives keep the home fires burning. But money may still be a cause of dissension.

There may be more money than ever before, as you move into the middle years, but it isn't the amount of money that's at issue. Rather, it's what you choose to do with it. Money may be a barometer of the way you feel about yourself, and the way you spend money or squirrel it away may tell the world a great deal about your self-image. Liz doesn't feel too good about herself as she moves into her fifties. Ken has gotten a promotion and is working harder than ever. He's seldom home, and when he is he's preoccupied by work he's brought home from the office. Liz, feeling unloved, has taken to spending. She doesn't make the connection, but there's a simple syllogism at work: She runs up bills until she provokes an argument with Ken; the argument is one way of grabbing attention, of screaming, "Look at me, I'm here."

Liz has money to spend because, although she's not earning an income of her own, Ken has never stinted. He has given her a checkbook, let her use his charge accounts. Other women are not so fortunate. There's the doctor's wife who must make do with $75 a week to feed and clothe a family of five. There's the wife without a key to the safe deposit box—and no knowledge of what's in that box. And there's the woman who wrote me the following letter: "I just found out that my husband named his mother as beneficiary of his life insurance. He says she'll give me the money if I need it, but shouldn't he name me?" Of course he should name her, if the money is meant for her. Why should a widow be dependent on the good will of her mother-in-law to collect on her husband's life insurance?

Some of these women remain trapped in unhappy marriages because they've never developed an independent means of support. They also have let money remain a mysterious male domain. They don't know how to obtain a charge account. They don't know much about banking. They don't know if their husbands have made investments, bought insurance, or written a will.

Others are in reasonably happy marriages, accepting a division of roles that makes them totally dependent on their husbands. These are often the women who are content with their lives . . . except for a lingering thought that receiving an "allowance" makes them too much like children. They're right. Both partners should share in family income, both partners should have funds to spend without accountability, both should consult when large sums need to be spent.

Because there is often not much discretionary spending money—either because there is not much money at all or because their husbands hold a tight rein—these are also the women who skim the household money. They may say "He gives me everything I want," yet they try to put aside a few dollars "just in case." A child might need help, a husband might have a birthday, the woman herself might want to travel to visit an ailing parent . . . it never hurts to have a few dollars tucked away. Some have more serious reasons. "After twenty-five years of marriage, I have reason to believe my husband is planning to leave," a woman told me. "It won't be right away, so I have a little time. How can I put money aside so he won't know I have it?"

The need for "secret funds" crops up over and over

again when women have no resources of their own. Keep
it in cash, open a savings account, buy Series EE bonds,
or invest in a mutual fund—women write to me and
want to know how, when interest is reported and they
pay taxes jointly with their husbands, they can keep any
money secret. In such situations, the best answer I can
offer is, buy EE bonds. They can be bought with as little
as $25 apiece and, while interest is taxable, it is not
reported or taxed until the bond is redeemed. Bonds can
be held for years, with no one the wiser, until the day
they are needed.

It's appalling that such subterfuge is needed in the
late 1980s. Perhaps it won't be needed much longer.
Women, whether they earn independent income or not,
are beginning to realize that they are entitled to spend
a share of the family income without accountability. They
are realizing that their own contribution to family maintenance has a dollar value. They are recognizing that
they are entitled to financial information. And they are
beginning to educate themselves in financial matters, so
that they will be able to share the burden with their
husbands and carry on for themselves when necessary.

Some men, after directing the family's financial fortunes for decades, are reluctant to share information with
their wives. With some, it's a deliberate effort to maintain
power. With others, it may be a reluctance to own up
to their own shortcomings. Bob, for instance, completely
agreed that family finances should be conducted as a
partnership. Yet, somehow, he kept postponing the actual
sit-down-and-share-the-information session. He was afraid
he'd be embarrassed, lose status in his wife's eyes, if she
saw that at times he hadn't managed so well.

And sometimes it's the wife who's reluctant. "I know
I *should* know what's going on, about the investments
and the insurance and all that," one long-married and
long-protected woman told me. "But I just tune it out
when Joe tries to tell me." Here, it's the wife who's
fearful of being found wanting, of seeming "dumb" about
finances. It's much easier to remain dependent. Sometimes, too, it's a wife who's fully in charge. The husband

turns over his income and she manages the family's financial fortunes. But probe beneath the surface, when it's a one-income husband-earning couple, and you'll almost always see that true power resides with the wage-earner. Francine Klagsbrun describes one such couple: Tom gives his pay to Peggy, who makes all the purchases, does all the investing. As Tom puts it: "She'll pick out a car or a TV set, and then I might come in and do a little bargaining with the owner. But basically, after she does the work, all I have to do is rubber-stamp it." That rubber stamp, as Klagsbrun says, "is the true indication of the nature of the economic power Peggy has. That is, it is power relegated to her by Tom. She does the research, lines up investments, makes purchases. But all her suggestions need Tom's approval because he is the source of the money and the final arbiter of how it will be spent. He is, in truth, the boss."

If you are a man who's accustomed to running your family financial affairs, wouldn't you like to share the burden of responsibility? Wouldn't you like to know that you've prepared your wife for whatever the future may hold? If you're a woman who has been sitting back, voluntarily or involuntarily, don't you think it's time you got involved? You'll be helping your husband, and yourself, by becoming informed. If your husband holds back, reluctant to "burden" you with financial information, point out that he'll be protecting you much more by providing you with the knowledge you'll need for survival if he isn't around. If he still refuses to talk, read some books on financial planning and attend some financial seminars. Banks and stock brokerage firms offer free programs, many specifically geared to women; adult education courses also abound. Your active interest may change your husband's mind. Even if it doesn't, you'll be better prepared to cope when coping is necessary.

Sudden Financial Change

"If only I could win a lottery," you might think, "then all my worries would be over." You may be surprised to hear it but coming into great wealth is not necessarily a cure-all. Somehow, we get used to functioning with the amount of money we have. We spend and save and relate to each other in terms of existing financial circumstances. Make a sudden sharp change in those circumstances, for better or for worse, and you upset accustomed ways of behaving.

Financial ups and downs alike, if they are sudden, can be stressful. On a list of stress-producing situations, widely circulated a few years ago, getting a raise was prominently featured along with losing your job. Just how much any of these events will affect you, as an individual and as a couple, depends on your own style of coping. Should you win a lottery, however, it will be nice to be prepared.

Handling a Windfall

For some people, it's winning a lottery. For others, it's coming into an inheritance. For still others, it's sudden and overwhelming success on the job. Whatever it is, it means a great deal more money. And more money, as wonderful as it is, may also create problems.

How do you think you would react if you win a lottery or receive an inheritance? Would you go on a spending spree? Sock the money away in investments for the future? Would your spouse go along with either course? Or would he or she have independent ideas? Many people who come into big money probably intend to retain much the same life-style, upgrading it a bit, but even these people sometimes find friendships eroding as a gulf seems to widen between the haves and the have-nots. Greediness sometimes sets in; witness the couple suing lifelong friends for a share of slot machine winnings. The issue: whose quarter was used for the winning play. Other people go off the deep end, quitting their jobs and running through many thousands of dollars in short order, although people who derive a sense of accomplishment from their work are likely to keep on working; blue-collar workers, at repetitive unfulfilling jobs, tend to quit when they get the opportunity. And some squirrel the money away, feeling that its very existence is enough; knowing that the money is available, even if it's never touched, lends security to their lives.

With any extreme of behavior, especially as it relates to money, a spouse can easily become upset and frustrated. "I thought Frank should keep his job, maybe just take a long vacation. But no, he had to quit. Now he spends all his time gambling, either at the track or in Vegas. He's not the same man I married—I wish he'd never won." Contrast that statement with this: "Now that we finally have money I'd like to buy a big house instead of this place. But he's afraid we'll show up our old friends if we move. What's the point of having money if you can't spend it?"

There may be special problems when the windfall is acquired, not through a gambler's luck, but through visible personal success—a flourishing legal career, a breakthrough to bestsellerdom, whatever. The spouse of someone who is suddenly a celebrity may feel neglected, overshadowed by the other's success . . . and a partnership that has been pulling together to reach a goal may splinter when one half of the team breaks the traces and spurts ahead. It may not exactly be jealousy, (although the green-eyed monster may rear its head); it may just be a feeling that the successful partner no longer needs the other. Indeed, the successful partner may be the one to pull away, seeking new relationships with people who know only the success and who don't "remember him when." When a relationship has been built upon mutual dependencies, as most are, a shift away from dependency by one partner can be devastating. It takes communication built on caring, a mutual wish for the relationship to survive, to weather the change.

Coping with Loss

The flip side of sudden gain is sudden loss, typically loss of a job. It's happening more and more these days, stemming from industrywide shutdowns in some fields, consolidations and mergers in others. It's a particular problem for older workers, who often find it difficult to land another job, and for women, whose in-and-out record of labor force participation puts them low on the seniority totem pole. But unemployment can hit anyone: young or old, male or female, black or white, blue-collar or professional. When it does, especially if it's through no fault of your own, the emotional fallout is as severe as the financial.

Studies have highlighted the emotional consequences of job loss; those emotional consequences have a ripple effect, from the individual to the entire family. Those emotional consequences also frequently have physical ramifications as well. A Johns Hopkins study pinpointed the correlation between unemployment and both physical and mental health. For each 1 percent rise in unemployment, M. Harvey Brenner found, suicides increase by 4.1 percent and homicides by 5.7 percent. Deaths from heart disease and cirrhosis of the the liver go up by 1.9 percent. And mental hospital admissions rise by 2.3 percent for women and by 4.3 percent for men.

The loss of a job, in short, is a major stressful event. It produces financial disruption, family strains, sometimes even the loss of friendships. More frequent and more violent family quarrels are reported in study after study. "At first, after Don was laid off, we were closer together. We were keeping a stiff upper lip in public, but needing each other's support in private. But lately, things have been awful. I'm working full-time and Don, although he's job-hunting, is so depressed that he's home a lot. When I get home, almost every night, he picks a fight. I don't know *what's* going to happen to us."

Self-esteem, not surprisingly, is often shattered by the loss of a job. Whether you goofed up, or the falling through of a major contract led to a general layoff, the tendency is to first blame the company—but second blame yourself. Whatever the reason, mental health professionals point out, the loss of a job is like any other loss, like a death in the family. It takes some time to recover, to move through a period of grief, and to move on.

Feelings of sadness, frustration, and anger, if allowed to linger, can disrupt your job search. They can also wreak havoc on your relationships with those nearest and dearest. If you're brimming with anger because you feel helpless in dealing with the situation, that anger may spill over on your spouse. And your spouse, if working, may feel unwanted resentment at bearing the entire financial burden. It's vitally important, although difficult at times like this, to talk through your feelings. Work out a stringent budget to get through the tough times, but talk about your situation. If you find yourselves bottled up by self-blame and frustration, look to a professional to help you weather the storm. There are community mental health clinics and family therapists in most communities; look in your local telephone book or call the nearest Family Service Agency for a referral. There are also informal self-help networks of unemployed men and women in many areas; these groups can bolster your spirits and also provide job leads.

You and Your Children

Experts on the family used to pontificate about the empty nest and the trauma it posed for mid-life couples. On the theory that married life centered around the children, they felt that married couples would lose their focus when children were grown. What would there be left to talk about? What would a mother do when her occupation had been child-rearing? Today the empty nest, instead of being a cause for concern, is a reason for celebration for many couples. "We love our children" as one mother puts it, "but we love them even more when they come to visit and leave again."

Fewer women today devote their entire lives to child-rearing. By the time children are in high school, if not before, most women return to the paid work force. If not, if they don't earn income, they are nonetheless busy

with vital activities of their own. The last thing they want
is full-time motherhood. Working or not, both mothers
and fathers relish the freedom and privacy and financial
independence that result when grown children are on
their own. Little wonder that a California study of 54
parents by psychologists Marjorie Fiske and David Chi-
riboga found that all but one looked forward with pleasure to the emptying of the nest.

The nest may be empty but the melody lingers on as
we face questions about how much we owe our grown
children. Should we give them money when they need
it, to subsidize their start-up incomes? Should we expect
them to live on their own but help them out with major
items such as graduate school or the purchase of a home?
Should such help, if given, be in the form of gifts or
loans? Should we deprive ourselves now, so that they
can inherit later? And, perhaps most important, do we
agree on just how much or how little we should do for
our adult offspring?

Some parents see the wisdom in helping children purchase a house but draw the line at lesser expenditures.
Some even insist on helping. "John and Nina could have
afforded the house they bought; they make more than I
do," says John's mother. "But they don't have much in
savings and those savings would have been down to a
few hundred dollars by the time they finished. I insisted
on loaning them the down payment, at no interest. They'll
pay me back when they've built their savings up again,
and it's just one of the things I think I should do for my
children."

Being able to do what she thinks she should do makes
John's mother a fairly typical member of this generation
of mid-life parents. Nearly half of the respondents to
Money magazine's 1985 survey expect to give their children financial help in buying a first home. Only 22 percent of the respondents received such help from their
own parents, many of whom were probably profoundly
affected by the Depression. Affluence definitely has an
impact on attitude.

But does giving (or lending) money give you any say

over how the money is spent? John's mother didn't expect veto power over the choice of a house, but some parents do. Some grown children accept financial help and then find that they are expected to consult on renovations . . . and, in some families, to extend a weekly dinner invitation. Such parents may be taking advantage of their children just as some children, with an advanced case of the "gimmes," take advantage of their parents. Whether financial help can and should be extended, or accepted, depends on the overall quality of the relationship. If there is healthy give-and-take between the generations, money is less likely to be misused.

Money-as-control is a major source of conflict between parents and their adult children, when conflict exists. It comes up in house-buying. And it crops up in other areas as well. In one of my favorite examples: For several years a New York stockbroker, taking advantage of estate and gift tax rules that allow him to reduce his taxable estate, has been giving each of his children $10,000 a year. After a few years one of his daughters, in an incident recounted in *The New York Times*, thanked him for his generosity and announced that she could now afford to have a baby as a single parent. The father was outraged and offended by this use of "his" money. The daughter replied that it was no longer his money; he had given it to her and it was hers to do as she saw fit.

More typically, dissension arises when money is offered but not yet given. Your 23-year-old daughter, for example, decides not to carry through on her resolve to become a lawyer; philosophy is now her first love. You promised to pay for law school, but you're not at all sure that a doctorate in philosophy is worth the cost. From your daughter's point of view, you're exerting unwarranted control over her life if you'll pay for one kind of schooling and not another. From another, equally valid point of view, it's your money and you have the right to decide whether it will be well spent.

It's true, of course, that you are not obligated to give your children anything, once they are grown. If you choose to do so, you are entitled to set limits, to have a

say in how the money is spent. But you're really not
entitled to be manipulative, to set up what psychologist
Howard Halpern calls a "double bind" situation in which
you urge independence but contrive to keep your children dependent. "One of the most common forms of the
double bind," Dr. Halpern writes in his book, *Cutting
Loose*, "is 'I want you to be self-reliant, so do as I say.' "
Or, as you might put it to your daughter, "I want you
to choose the career that's right for you, but there is no
future in being a philosophy professor." You don't have
to pay for graduate school—but don't imply that she
can't choose her own career. Try to give, if you choose
to do so, without strings attached.

Your child may want help that you are unwilling to
give, with or without strings. "He seems to think we
owe it to him; we don't agree." Or your child, in the
interests of independence, may reject help that you
urgently want to give. "It's so expensive to live in New
York, but Arlene insists that she has to do it on her own.
I tried sending her checks without discussing it, but she
just tore them up." Either way, it's emotions that are at
issue rather than money, emotions that are even more
complicated if parents disagree. "I think we *should* pay
for Andy's grad school, whatever he chooses to study.
My wife won't have it; she thinks it's up to us to curb
Andy's foolishness. But when do they grow up, if we
keep babying them into their mid-twenties?"

Some young adults are immature, unable to break
loose from parental support. They may seek degree after
degree in various fields, postponing entry into the real
world. Or they may repeatedly complain that interestng
jobs don't pay enough money. With these children you
have a valid question: "Won't it be better for *him* if we
push him out of the nest so he is forced to fly?" Ongoing
financial support, you may well believe, will simply prevent such a child from growing up. But whatever you
decide to do, whether your grown child succeeds in flying
or not, don't consider yourself a failure as a parent. You
can only do so much.

Some young adults have crossed the bridge to independence but need temporary parental help until they reach a well-defined goal. "Debbie was getting her MBA part-time, with help from her employer. But the company merged into another and she lost her tuition benefits along with her job. We want her to finish the degree, so we agreed to pay for it. She'll pay us back."

It can be a question of values. It's easier for some parents to support a medical student than an aspiring playwright. "Twenty years ago I gave him a penny a week for bubble gum. Then it was allowance money, summer camp, college tuition. When does it stop?" an angry father said to *McCall's* magazine some years back. "If the boy needed something important," he says of his son, a would-be painter, "I'd give it to him of course. If he'd get even a part-time job, I'd help out. But at twenty-three, just to keep *asking . . .* " Other parents are willing to subsidize the trying out of a dream, at least for a couple of years. "If he gets caught up in making a living, before he ever gets to see whether he can make it as a playwright, he'll always regret it," said one mother. "And so will we, if we don't at least give him the chance."

The way parents feel about the matter may have a great deal to do with their children's attitude. If the children feel they have it coming to them, that we *owe* them whatever they want well into adulthood, we may very well rebel. After all, these years should be ours. We've paid our dues. But you never give up being a parent. And you never find it easy to turn your back on a child, of any age, who needs help. The best way to resolve the matter, if you decide to help, is to get all the cards out on the table. Make it very clear how much help you are willing to give, for how long, and on what basis. Then it's up to the child to accept, or to refuse.

When Children Come Home Again

It's hard enough figuring out what to do about grown children's need for financial help when they're living on their own. But what do you do when they come home again? With low entry-level salaries in many fields, coupled with the high cost of housing in urban areas, many empty-nesters are finding the chicks coming home to roost. Some of these chicks find the nest too comfortable to leave, with some of the "young adults" living in the parental home these days ranging into their mid- and upper thirties. Some move out, then in again, through what seems to be a revolving door. "Three out of our four are living here now," says a New Jersey woman. "Sometimes it's two, sometimes it's all four. But in the last eight years, since the youngest finished college, we haven't had the house to ourselves at all."

Sometimes the returnees have children of their own. In one case it's a young family saving money to buy a house. In another it's divorced children seeking both babysitting and financial support until they get back on their feet. Whatever the reason for children's return, both generations have adjustments to make.

Some of the adjustments are physical. "When David moved out, I set up his room as my computer center," says a free-lance writer. "Now he's announced that he's coming back, and I have to move all my equipment." Some of the adjustments are financial. "If he's only going to be here for a couple of months, I don't mind treating him like a guest. When he stays on and on, I think he should pitch in and, at the very least, pay for the food he consumes." And some of the adjustments are emotional. "We had gotten used to having all the privacy we wanted, to eating dinner when we wanted to and making love when we wanted to. Now, all of a sudden," says one mother wistfully, "the kids are home again."

Many of the problems center around something it's extremely difficult to avoid: falling back into familiar parent-child roles. It's only natural for you to assert authority as parents when a child moves back under your own roof, even if it's inappropriate to ask a 27-year-old where he's going and with whom. It's only natural for your children to fall back into dependency when they move back, to let you pick up after them, do their laundry, and cook their meals. It's natural, but it isn't healthy. Don't keep your grown child dependent emotionally just because he or she is dependent financially. Don't *let* your grown child become dependent emotionally just because he or she needs financial help. Set the ground rules in advance, on an adult-to-adult basis: How long is the stay expected to last. What will the child contribute to the household?

One couple solves the contribution question by keeping track of household expenses, then dividing total costs among the number of people resident at any one time. The parents pay half the costs; whether two or three or four adult children are in residence, they split the other half. This doesn't seem to be a popular route. More parents accept token contributions toward room and board, on the theory that the child needs to build a nest egg toward moving out. This becomes harder to justify, though, when parents see that same child spending freely on social life. One practical idea, for the child who seems to have moved in on a long-range basis: Ask for a percentage of income (20 to 25 percent) towards "rent." You may save some of that money and return it to your child on move-out day; you may actually apply it toward your household expenses. Either way, your child will feel like an adult and a contributing member of the household.

Whatever you decide to do, however, decide it jointly. You and your spouse should have a pre-move-in conference to decide your own expectations, then have a conference with your offspring to make those expectations clear. Don't put yourselves in a situation where one of you expects a contribution toward room and board while the other offers the child an allowance. Don't have one of you indulging the child, slipping money under the table, while the other becomes resentful. Don't ever put a child, especially a grown child, in the position of playing one of you off against the other. And, if you find that your lives are being unreasonably and permanently disrupted by the presence of your adult child, set a time limit for that child's moving out. It may be preferable to

subsidize an apartment elsewhere if absolutely necessary
than to have a grownup child underfoot.

Married Children

Complications are always multiplied by the number
of people involved in a given situation. There are plenty
of adjustments to make when a single adult child moves
back in. But there are even more adjustments when that
child has a spouse and/or a child along for the ride. When
three generations are involved, you may feel put upon
as an unpaid babysitter. "At first I was delighted to spend
time with my granddaughter," Doris says. "It gave us a
chance to get acquainted while my daughter was out job-
hunting. But lately I feel she's been taking advantage of
me. I want to get on with my own life, and I'm not sure
what to do about it."

What cuts many parents to the quick, whether babysitting or cash gifts are at issue, is an apparent lack of
appreciation. "They act as if they've got it coming to
them, as if somehow we never did do enough for them
or can do enough for them. When do they grow up? And
when do we get to live our lives?" When children have
this attitude, therapists observe, it may be a matter of
emotional need. Some children are simply reluctant to
grow up. If this seems to be the case with your children,
remind yourself that it isn't doing your child any favors
to keep that child dependent. Then work together with
the child to seek solutions. "What kind of child care do
you think will be best for Suzie?" may work better than
a flat-out, "I'm not available for any more babysitting."
But be prepared to stand firm. You will always be emotionally involved with your children, but you needn't
always be financially involved.

Financial support of married children, even when those
children are living independently, is always tricky. You
may want to help your married children over some rough
spots to make life a bit easier. They may fiercely resent
what they see as interference, as treating them like chil-

dren. One young bride was terribly upset when, in opposition to her expressed request, her mother-in-law stocked the newlyweds' refrigerator before they returned from their honeymoon. Another turned down theater tickets that looked like a handout, even though it meant skipping an outing that included the rest of the family. Sometimes children are supersensitive (especially when they are young, married right out of school), and sometimes parents are, but it *is* difficult to give gifts without appearing to be intrusive. It's particularly difficult at the outset, before the independence of the newly married couple is well established. And it's particularly upsetting when son- or daughter-in-law objects. "My husband was terribly upset when my parents bought expensive things for our house, things we couldn't yet afford to buy for ourselves. He thought it was a reflection on his abilities. I didn't understand how he felt for a long time," says this woman who's now been married for a decade; "when I did, although I didn't see any harm in the gifts, I put a stop to them."

The problem with giving and taking, of course, is that it's seldom a purely objective transaction. You may think there are no strings attached, but most loving children will tend to react to gifts with an eagerness to please, an eagerness they will then resent. Most loving parents, in turn, will have lingering feelings that adult children really ought to be independent. Listen to the signals in your own relationships, then proceed accordingly.

As Parents Age

As children's needs can press in on your middle years, so can the needs of aging parents. It's a question of demographics, as more people live longer. More and more families, in fact, now consist of four generations, with retirees caring for the elderly. You may be nowhere near retirement, in these middle years of life, but you may very well have aging parents turning to you with emotional and/or financial needs.

Age alone does not equal dependency. Our parents are not only living longer, they are living healthy independent lives well into their seventies and eighties and sometimes beyond. Gerontologists now identify at least two separate stages of aging. There are the "young-old," those in vigorous health up to age 75 or so. And there are the "old-old," those over 75 or 80 who are beginning to fail. Some specialists in aging look at three stages, with "old age" not setting in until the mid-eighties. With people over age 85 now numbering 2.6 million, this is the group called the "extreme aged" or the "oldest old."

Your role as a child will differ with these stages of aging in your parents. While you're in your forties and fifties, you and your parents are likely to be leading your own independent lives. You'll relate to each other in much the same way you always have—personality traits don't fade, if anything they become exaggerated with age—but lurking dependency may alter the tone. By the time you are nearing retirement, your parents may be in real need and you may be confronting issues of nursing home care, Medicare, and a transfer of assets to ensure Medicaid eligibility. When you reach this stage, or even before, you would do well to consult an attorney specializing in problems of the elderly.

Meanwhile, as parents begin to feel their age, you may be caught up in their need for emotional support. For example: Do you have an aging parent who threatens to withhold your inheritance if you (a) don't visit or call often enough, (b) move to a distant city, or (c) don't send the grandchildren for periodic visits? Whether such threats are made seriously or in jest, they are a way of keeping you involved with your parent. "Using the inheritance as a tool," says psychotherapist Ellen Mendel, "can be a controlling way of saying, 'Don't leave,' 'Take care of me.' Such parents can't bear to look helpless so they show their authority via the power of the purse, via threats over the inheritance."

More typical, however, is the older parent on a fixed income who won't discuss money with you at all. You'd like to help but don't know if help is needed or, if it is, how your parent will feel about taking it from you. Now the issue of control may be in your hands. If you insist on knowing your parent's financial situation, if you insist on providing a stipend, you may foster a sense of helplessness. Don't. If you're sure that extra help would come in handy and that your parent isn't living modestly out of choice, then provide help in specific ways. Buy a new water heater if one is needed, rather than offending your parents by mailing a check (unless, in fact, regular cash support is vital).

You may suspect that your mother would have enough to live on if only she didn't insist on stashing her money in passbook savings in that nice solid bank across the street. You can try to introduce her to more sophisticated financial vehicles—Treasury bills, for example, or money market mutual funds—but be prepared for resistance. Old habits die hard. And you may be accused of interfering where it's none of your business.

Then there's the parent who does have some money tucked away. At least you're pretty sure she does. But now she's asking for help. "We couldn't ask Mom about her savings so we helped her, even though it was a real drain just when our own kids were in college. Then," Anne says with some irritation, "it turned out that she did have money after all. She left each of her grandchildren $3,000." It was important to this grandmother, as it is to many, that she be remembered with love. But Anne might have told her, with love, that the money meant more earlier. She might even have suggested a direct gift from grandmother to grandchildren, designated for college, during her lifetime.

If you've never talked openly about money with your parents, however, it may be almost impossible to start now. Your parents may never tell you how well they are managing, never mention an inheritance, never even let you know whether they've made a will. If they tell you, they fear they'll lose control over their own affairs. If you ask, they may accuse you of prying.

Independence is an important source of self-esteem; it is especially important for the elderly, who may fiercely resent interference in their affairs. A woman who has always handled the family finances does not want to have you take over just because she's getting older. A widower, contemplating remarriage, does not want to hear his children say, "She's only after your money." He may well conclude that it is his children who are after his money.

Treading carefully is the order of the day when it comes to offering help to elderly parents, or curtailing their independence in any way. In a survey taken by the American Association of Retired Persons and the National Retired Teachers Association, reported in *Dynamic Years*, respondents said, in essence:

- We want—and need—emotional rather than financial support.
- We want involvement, participation, communication.
- We want to continue sharing our lives with you, and we would like you to share your lives with us.
- We want—so long as it is financially and physically possible—to maintain our independence.

There may well come a time, however, when your parents need more than emotional support, when they are unable to function completely on their own. Now the going can get really sticky, for both generations, because a need for independence—or, at least, a feeling of being in charge of one's own affairs—doesn't diminish just because financial help is needed. Do what you can to sustain your parent's autonomy, by not taking over. Don't even give advice about resolving a conflict or where to live or anything else; give opinions, when asked, but not advice. If you give advice, whether it works or not, the responsibility—and the problem itself—becomes yours. Respect your parents' privacy, too, and don't ask about what you don't need to know. Involve your parents in decision-making that affects their lives. And stick to the real issues in your discussions, things that matter now; don't dredge up the past.

A feeling of independence may be vitally important to the elderly who actually need help. When one healthy and active woman in her eighties (still working part-time) was hit by a car and broke her hip, she was immobilized. She was also bitterly angry at her situation. Although she is close to her children, she refuses to tell them anything about her financial affairs . . . and they need to know to help her make appropriate decisions about the rehabilitative care she needs. She's lost some control over her own life simply by being laid up; she'll lose more, she feels, if she shares financial information with her children.

"We think of older people as frail and childlike," notes Rona Bartelstone, a Florida-based social worker who specializes in meeting the needs of retired adults and their faraway children. "You don't get to be eighty or ninety by being weak and frail, but by being survivors, strong and independent and capable. It's important to recognize these strengths in parents and to see that relinquishing that strength means giving up self-respect. Most older people do not want to depend on their children."

Sometimes, of course, help is necessary, either because a parent is ill and unable to manage financial affairs or because there simply isn't enough money. Then, if the relationship has been a good one over the years, it should be possible to talk openly. If either of you finds it hard to deal with each other as adults (and there are always lingering remnants of the parent-child relationship, no matter how old you are), then talk about money may skirt the real issues. There may be conflict, especially if conflict has been part of the pattern all along. If you feel, deep down, that your parents never quite let go and let you live your own life, for example, or if you suspect your parents of favoring a brother or sister, tensions may erupt when the elderly parent needs help.

"Money hang-ups between generations are widespread and rest on more than economic considerations," say Jane Otten and Florence D. Shelley in *When Your Parents Grow Old*. "The entire quality of a lifetime relationship is involved, and even good rapport can become strained during discussions about money—especially when questions revolve around how much who is going to spend on what, how much will come from the parent or the child, how much will be left to the child."

If you have brothers and sisters you'll probably find that one of you, whether for reasons of geography or of personality, will assume primary responsibility. This "caretaker" child may resent, and in turn be resented by, the others. Sometimes, indeed, it's the caretaker who receives criticism from the aging parent, while an absent sibling is repeatedly praised. Here's where behavior stereotypes often come into play. A son fulfills his obligations, in many families, by tending to financial affairs; a daughter is expected to provide physical care, to tend to the house, provide meals, chauffeur the parent to the doctor. But today's daughters are, often as not, working full-time. Being pushed and pulled among the demands of your job, your spouse, and your parents can create intolerable strain.

When a parent begins to need this much help, you may face severe problems based solely on geographic distance: Your parents may have retired to Florida, for example, while you live in Connecticut. Or they may have stayed in the home town in Iowa while you moved to Oregon. In such a situation—or in the situation where you live nearby but can't provide full-time care—many communities have resources that can help. From telephone reassurance programs to Meals on Wheels, there are free or low-cost programs. From live-in companions to housekeepers to nurses, there is no limit to the care that money can buy. Geriatric consultants, members of a new profession meeting a growing need, can help to find necessary services if you can't find them on your own; these consultants usually charge an hourly fee for services that range from running errands to arranging medical care.

Some overburdened middle-aged couples find that they can, in one writer's words, "trade money for emotional elbow room," buying the services that elderly parents need. Yet some elderly parents won't let money be spent on them—perhaps because giving money is not quite the same, in their eyes, as giving love. Giving money can be a way of assuaging guilt while staying away from any direct involvement in a parent's life. Ideally, whatever money you give should be an expression of your love—and your parents should see your love as well.

When considerable amounts of either money or time are devoted to an elderly parent's care, however, your own marriage may suffer. The most selfless spouse may begin to resent a long-term drain on your emotions, and therefore on his. The most devoted spouse may see money saved for your own retirement, and time hoarded for your own mid-life rewards, flowing out in an endless stream.

There's no real resolution to these problems, but it can help to plan ahead. If possible, try to get things out in the open with your parents before they begin to ail or become dependent. Will they have the resources to cope with a long illness? Where would they prefer to live? Will they give you a durable power of attorney, now, that can be invoked if they become unable to manage their own affairs? (Your parent's doctor can be designated to determine when the power of attorney goes into effect; a banker or lawyer can be named to act with you on financial matters.)

Then, if you face what so many mid-life people must face in this age of medical miracles—an aging and increasingly dependent parent—accept your own limitations, without guilt. You cannot do everything for your parent now, any more than you can reshape your relationship with your parents in the past. You may be sad about your inability to do more for your parents, to stave off death if you could, but you should not feel guilty.

Mid-Life Money Traps

• Today's mid-life generation is caught between tradition and innovation, between accepted roles and new rules. Relationships in such a time of transition are subject to strain and require special care.

• Marriage can fall victim to sudden changes—on the job front or at home—if husbands and wives fail to adapt. Communication skills are essential to adaptation. Don't keep resentments to yourself. Don't expect your husband or wife to know that something is bothering you, or what that something is. Don't bottle up irritations until they explode. Tell your spouse when something is wrong in a nonaccusatory way, so that you can resolve your differences.

• If you offer financial help to grown children (and whether you do or not is up to you), try to do so without being manipulative. Make the terms of the offer clear and then stand back. Whatever you do, don't let the demands of adult children put a strain on your finances or drive a wedge between you and your spouse.

• As your parents age, roles may be reversed and they may become emotionally and financially dependent on you. Before this happens try, without intruding, to ascertain the extent of financial need. Try to help them remain independent as long as possible. And help them, when your involvement is inescapable, retain both privacy and dignity.

· 9 ·

The Later Years

THE LATER years bring new concerns, both financial and emotional. Your family may be growing, as children marry and produce children of their own. Your outer world may seem to be shrinking as you contemplate retirement. You may look forward to leaving the work force, perhaps at an early age, to do all the things you've dreamed of doing. You may dread retirement as a forced putting-out-to-pasture, especially if you derive much of your identity from the work you do and the income you earn. However you feel about it and however old or young you are at the time, retirement itself may shift an accustomed frame of reference, making it necessary to become reacquainted with spouse and children and, often, to readjust longstanding financial habits.

Have *you* anticipated retirement? Have you planned in realistic terms for the amount of time you may well spend in those postworking years? The average 65-year-old man now lives another fourteen years; the average 65-year-old woman can anticipate nineteen years of life. Many, both men and women, live considerably longer. At the same time, many are choosing to retire early, expanding the years spent in retirement. Where almost 80 percent of men ages 55 to 64 were in the work force in 1973, fewer than 70 percent were in the work force in 1983. Whether you choose to retire early or not, the retirement years are years worth planning for, not simply taking one at a time. Or you may find yourself, in the words of one 81-year-old man, saying, "If I'd known I was going to live this long, I would have done something besides play golf."

What do *you* want to do in retirement? What does your spouse want to do? Are your ideas similar, or very far apart? You may have some serious accommodations to make . . . if you're dreaming of fishing the days away at a Vermont lake, while your partner wants to laze in the warmth of the Florida sun . . . if you want to retire and your spouse plans to keep on working . . . if you want to do meaningful volunteer work while your spouse wants you as a daily bridge partner . . . if you want to stay put, in a familiar community, while your spouse longs to pull up stakes and move . . . if you expect to enjoy retirement, living up to the money you've saved, while your spouse thinks it necessary to pinch pennies to the end. You may have to ask what your spouse does want and expect. Making assumptions, if you've never discussed the issues, can be dangerous.

As you get closer to retirement, you'll be forced to take a close look at your finances: pensions, Social Security, estate planning. You will also want to think about your personal plans: What you will do in retirement (travel? volunteer work? take courses? seek a part-time post-retirement job?) and where you will do it (that Vermont cottage? a Florida condominium? where you are right now?). And you should give some thought to the people in your life, as all of your retirement decisions will affect those people and your relationships with them.

When to Retire

Mandatory retirement is, in most fields, a thing of the past. You may therefore choose to stay on the job. You'll be likely to make this choice if you derive a great deal of pleasure from what you do and, particularly, if you're self-employed and able to make your own rules. If your job is repetitive and uninteresting, on the other hand, and if you have a decent pension, you may have had quite enough of the working life by the time you reach age 55 or 60. Whatever you decide to do, do it in the context of your anticipated retirement income, your plans for the use of retirement time, and the feelings of your spouse.

One of the first considerations, if you and your spouse are both employed, is whether or not you should retire simultaneously. Since you may be of different ages, and since a wife may have entered the work force considerably later than her husband, this is a serious issue. "We've been looking forward for years to the day when we could travel without worrying about vacation schedules; we want to take a freighter, without thinking about what day or week we'll return, and see where we wind up. How can we do that if I retire and Nell keeps on working?" Nell, however, is not sure what she wants to do: "Yes, we've planned on traveling, and I'm sorely tempted. But I didn't go back to work until our girls were all in school and it took me a long time to move ahead. Now I'm doing really interesting work and I'm not sure I'm ready to retire."

The question isn't simple, and there are no simple solutions. If George retires and Nell keeps right on working, they will have to defer their travel plans. He's 65 now, healthy and active, and eager to go. Will he be as eager in five years? If Nell keeps on working, the family income—and savings toward travel—will be greater. But George, unwilling to wait and to occupy himself while Nell is at work, may urge Nell to retire. If she does, how will it work out in the long run? The freighter trip may be fun but, when it is over, what will take the place of the job she loved? Will she and George make a satisfactory new life or will she be left with a sense of frustration at her incomplete career? If Nell is widowed before she herself has reached retirement age, as is, unfortunately, quite possible, will her grief be worse because she has lost not only George but her own job, on-the-job friends, and income as well? Or will she be sorrier if she kept on working, and they never had the trip they planned?

You'll have to make your own decision when faced with such a question. But whether you decide to retire together or not and whether, in fact, you are both working or not, don't be surprised by changes in your relationship. Retirement brings changes, not least of which, for many, is a loss of perceived status going along with loss of income. Where marital power has been a function of breadwinning, power shifts may be radical. The process of aging brings changes too. The sex roles inculcated by our society—men are independent, unemotional, and brave; women are dependent, sentimental, and timid—tend to blur with the years. Men frequently become more sensitive in later life, more tuned in to feelings. One sign of this change is that family and friends become increasingly important with the years. Women, at the same time, often become more independent and assertive.

This blurring of accustomed sex role behavior can bring you closer together—unless either of you fights to retain rigid sex role characteristics. The woman who has learned to extract money from her husband by appealing to his thrifty instincts, letting him feel that he's made the decision to seek a particular bargain, may decide she no longer wants to play games. Unless he has mellowed, they will be in for some conflict—and it's possible that neither will understand why. On another front, women will dispute which is worst: the retired husband who doesn't lift a finger around the house or the retired husband who intrudes on every moment of her day, shifting his power base from job to home by telling her how to do things she's been doing perfectly well for forty years.

Marriage in the later years is not played by the same rules as marriage in the early and middle years. Even if you've had a long and solid relationship with the person you married thirty or forty years ago, be prepared for some subtle shifts in your relationship as you enter retirement.

Money Issues

Sex roles may blur, but some personality attributes stiffen with age. The adamant young man becomes the stubborn old man; the penny-pinching young woman becomes the miserly old woman. You'll find, as you move into the retirement years, that money hang-ups of the past may come back to haunt you in the present. Jack and Adele, as an example, have had many disagreements over money in their forty-one years of marriage, disagreements which almost fractured the marriage on more than one occasion. Jack, accusing Adele of extravagance, doled out money over the years, especially in the beginning, and insisted on an accounting of every penny. Adele, accusing Jack of miserliness, saved from her household allowance so that she could spend a little on the children and, later, on herself. Their arguments over money, heated in the early years, finally subsided as income grew and responsibilities diminished. Now, as Jack becomes nervous about impending retirement, tension is building again. And tension of any sort, in this family, erupts in a battle over money.

Money does represent security. True, of course, up to a point, but how much money makes you really secure? How much money cushions you against illness? How much retirement income will be enough? An "adequate" retirement income, like an adequate preretirement income, is subject not only to a financial yardstick but to your own perception. You may think you're in financial hot water and actually be in over your head; you may, like Jack, think you're in trouble and not be at all.

Your life will change in retirement. It will change because, very likely, there is less money. And it will change, if you let it, because of fears about the adequacy of your income. Old anxieties, as we've seen, can emerge to generate new conflicts. Look at your own needs, both practical and psychological. If your life-style demands more money, you will need more money. If prestige rides on visible wealth, you will want more money. If your emotional state requires a large financial security blanket, then you will not feel comfortable with less. If a reduction in income makes you worry, even if what's still coming in is compatible with your spending patterns, you will worry. If a cessation of earned income makes you nervous, even if you have more than enough stashed away to last your lifetime and more, you will be nervous. Budgets and statistical data and financial projections have nothing to do with it. You can and should figure out your retirement finances, but do so recognizing that "enough" is not altogether a rational concept. How much you need depends, to a very large extent, on how much you think you need. Two people can, in theory, have identical needs and identical income to meet those needs. One will feel secure, the other will be anxious.

People have different feelings about money. And people have different approaches to money management, personality-related methods of coping with the complexities of finance. How do you handle money? Have you always been prudent, keeping track of expenditures and squirreling money away for the rainy future? If so, you are demonstrating self-reliance—but you may panic at the thought of retirement. Or are you casually philosophical about money, not worrying too much because "I've always managed"? If so, psychologist would say, you are more secure. With faith in the way the world has always treated you, you don't see much need to worry—but you may be refusing to face facts. Either trait, of course, can be taken to an extreme. Prudence can become a compulsion to save, an unreasoning fear of the future. A happy-go-lucky approach can lead to unwise spending, to the accumulation of bills that, once income is reduced, cannot easily be paid.

If you are married, you must come to terms not only with your own attitudes but with those of your spouse. You may have come to terms long ago, recognizing and accepting different ingrained attitudes toward money. "I've always been more willing to spend, Arthur to save. We balance each other." But that hard-won balance may

be tested anew if the prospect of retirement represents
a strain to both your budget and your emotions. That
strain may reactivate differences you thought long settled. "Arthur always said long-distance telephone calls
were an extravagance, but I finally convinced him that
it was the nicest way to keep in touch with the children,
and a way we really could afford. But now that retirement
is looming over his shoulder, he's going back to his old
thinking and yelling if I make a call. The phone bill gives
him apoplexy. He can't believe that we won't die broke."

Sometimes the balance is jeopardized by changing circumstances: Arthur has a justifiable if exaggerated concern. Sometimes it is threatened by inability to adjust
to new facts of life: Financial security may have been
attained but the habit of saving is too strong to break.
"I'm a poor girl who will always be a poor girl," says a
publisher, a woman approaching 60 who has received a
financial windfall but can't seem to spend it. "I can't
change now." She is not alone, not in this generation.
You probably have spent much of your adult life, influ-
enced by your parents' and perhaps your own memories
of the Depression, watching your pennies. First you had
to ensure a reasonable standard of living for your family,
then you had to put the children through school, then
save for your own retirement. It's not easy to break the
habit, even when the long-sought goal is at hand: the
Depression is over, the children are grown, and your
retirement is now.

If only one of you has the saving habit, you may have
a conflict on your hands. "My wife finds it more difficult
than I do to get out of the habit of saving; she can't seem
to realize how well off we are and how few years we have
in which to enjoy our assets." If both of you still feel
compelled to save, there may be no conflict but you may
be depriving yourselves of a richly deserved retirement.
Life may, of course, be longer than you think. Runaway
inflation may intermittently rear its ugly head. But if
you've assured an adequate retirement income, try to
relax and enjoy it. Don't be the recluse, living close to

the bone, who leaves cash and bankbooks for others to
find. Don't be the self-sacrificing parent, living near the
poverty line in order to leave money to children and
grandchildren. Don't be like the couple who saved for
years, planning a postretirement trip around the world,
only to go into an emotional tailspin when it came to
actually taking the trip: "We'd have to spend so much
money . . . what if we need it later?"

Money Plans

The way to find out how much money you'll actually
have in retirement, of course, is to plan ahead. That
means joint planning, if you're married, to maximize
retirement income and minimize outgo. It also means
sharing information about the financial facts of your lives.
There are plenty of good books available on financial
planning for retirement; I'll focus this discussion, therefore, on the areas that are likely to affect your relationship.

Information Please

Newlyweds frequently start out sharing money management chores; then, as time goes by, the partner who
is either more willing or more competent generally takes
over. The one-sided nature of money management in
many families, combined with stereotypes that find many
older men managing the money while their wives manage the home, frequently leaves survivors in serious trouble. Men suffer more in losing the nurturing and
companionship provided by their wives, because they
are less likely than women to have other warm relationships. The death rate of widowers—unless they remarry—
is higher than average for their age bracket. Women have
more friends, as a rule, and are better equipped to go
on emotionally after being widowed, but they often have
less financial know-how. Older widows, especially, shel-
tered by their husbands from the financial facts of life,

are too often left high and dry, prey to the self-serving advice of charlatans. Even with good advice, not knowing what the assets are and where they are can add unreasonably to grief. "It took me nearly two years after the death of my husband to fit together the puzzle of exactly what we owned," a widow wrote to *Retirement Living* magazine, "who to get information from, and how to continue in the areas he 'took care of'—finances, house, car, and general life-style. Husbands have a way of putting you off with 'later' or 'don't worry about that now.' *Do* worry about these things! Force your husband to sit down and explain everything. It's not being morbid or pessimistic—just plain common sense."

The stereotypes may be reversed—sometimes it's a widower who's left ignorant of the family's finances—but, if you don't want to leave your survivor in trouble, resenting you instead of revering you, take the time to share necessary information now. Don't shy away, as some couples do, out of a reluctance to think about death; 70 percent of wives outlive their husbands and desperately need the information. Don't clam up out of mistrust, wanting to conceal assets in the event of divorce. A sharp divorce lawyer can probably ferret out any major assets you try to hide; a good estate lawyer may be able to do the same, but it will cost your survivor both time and money. And don't hold back because you assume your spouse won't understand finances or simply isn't interested; your control of the situation now will penalize your survivor later. Interested or not, there are things you both need to know:

• The whereabouts of important papers: wills, insurance policies, deeds, marriage licenses, birth certificates and adoption papers, divorce decrees, military discharge papers, income tax returns and supporting papers, important bills of sale, and records of ownership. Write down your employment histories, too, together with any information you may have about job-related benefits. Sometimes pension payments may be due under a previous job, or life insurance under an old policy.

• Names and addresses of personal advisers: accountant, lawyer, insurance agent, stockbroker, financial planner. It's a good idea, in fact, to meet these important people as a couple.

• An up-to-date list (reviewed periodically) of assets and liabilities, together with details on mortgages and other loans and payment due dates, the location of bank accounts and safe deposit boxes, plus the location of bankbooks and safe deposit key.

• Anticipated retirement income from all sources, as well as projected outgo.

• Important household information: the location of appliance warranties, names and addresses of repair services, schedules of any annual repair contracts.

You'll be very glad to have all of this information should your partner die or become disabled. You'll need other information, as well, should you move into retirement together.

Pensions

If you will receive a pension—about half of all private employees and three-quarters of government civilian employees do—you will have some choices to make. There are two choices, in particular, that you and your spouse should make together.

Dependent protection, that is, benefits for your survivor, is perhaps the most important, a choice that, if poorly made, can lead to conflict now and bitterness later. Actually, as a worker, you don't have as much choice as you used to have. Under prior law an employee had complete control over the pension; workers could, and many did, elect to receive a larger pension during their lifetimes at the cost of leaving their survivors without any monthly pension benefits at all. Since most workers were men, and most survivors women, and since men on the average die before women do, this led to a large number of impoverished elderly women. Pension "reforms" that made a joint and survivor form of pension

automatic unless the employee elected otherwise did not
do the trick; a great many men simply never discussed
the matter with their wives and elected the larger individual pension. "I heard there was a new law that guaranteed me part of Joe's pension," says one widow. "Some
law. After he died, just two years into retirement, I found
out I got nothing at all."

Under current legislation, Joe couldn't get away with
unilateral action. Today a joint and survivor annuity, with
regular payments made to your spouse after your death,
is automatic under pension law unless you *both* agree,
in writing, to make another choice. Depending on the
terms of your particular plan, there may be several alternatives: (1) Joint and survivor payments may be made
according to different calculations. You might elect identical payments to yourself and to your survivor (which
will, of course, reduce payments during your lifetime),
or you might elect that the survivor receive 50 percent
of your payments (which will also reduce your lifetime
payments, but not as much). (2) A "period certain" form
would limit payments to your lifetime, except that payments would in any case be made for a minimum guaranteed period; a typical period would be ten years. (3)
An individual or life annuity would end at your death.
Although a life annuity will provide larger monthly payments than a joint and survivor annuity, election of this
option means that you are gambling on outliving your
spouse . . . and on his or her ability to survive economically without either you or your pension.

The choice you make will depend, at least in part, on
your other sources of retirement income. But I urge you,
whatever your income level, to make the choice together.

Consider it carefully, and recognize the law's limitations. An employee can no longer take early retirement
without a spouse's consent. And no married employee,
man or woman, now has a unilateral right to decide either
the beneficiary of the pension or its form of payment.
Where a worker has been separated for many years, but
not legally divorced, that worker must secure that spouse's

written consent to pension provisions. "You mean I can't designate my children as beneficiaries of my pension?" a woman asks in disbelief. "I've been separated from that so-and-so for twenty years, and he can take the pension from my children?" That's exactly what can happen.

Lump sum or monthly benefits may be another option. It should be apparent that if you elect to receive a lump sum distribution at retirement, there will be no later payments of any kind to your survivor. There may not even be adequate money for your lifetime, unless you do very well at investing that lump sum. "Oh, he was a genius, he was. He knew just how to make a killing in the market. But the market went down just as we needed the money, and there went his killing," Rita complains to a friend, as her husband listens expressionlessly. "We wanted to travel, but I guess now we'll stick pretty close to home."

Lump sum payouts make more sense, as a rule, for people in upper-income brackets. Before you decide which is best for you, a lump sum distribution or regular monthly payments, consider (in conjunction with your spouse): (1) What rate of return would you have to earn on your lump sum to give you the monthly payments you would otherwise receive from the pension? Can you realistically expect to earn this rate of return even if interest rates decline? (2) Is your pension an essential part of your retirement income, needed for survival? If so, take the regular monthly payments so that you eliminate any risk of outliving your income. (3) A lump sum distribution is not equivalent to your annual pension multiplied by your life expectancy; instead it is reduced by the interest the company would otherwise earn on the unpaid portion. You are more likely to come out ahead with a lump sum payment if this figure, your company's "discount rate," is less than current investment yields.

Individual Retirement Accounts

If you've been smart you've been putting money into an IRA each year, at least since the law was changed to permit any worker, covered by a company pension or not, to do so. (Under 1986 tax legislation, the law may revert to the previous requirement wherein only those not covered by a pension plan are eligible. Existing accounts may continue to accrue interest on a tax-deferred basis.) As you approach retirement, this is what you should know:

• IRA funds may be withdrawn without tax penalty after you reach age 59½. Withdrawal must start by April 1 of the year after you reach age 70½. You may continue contributing to an IRA until age 70½, as long as you are earning income, even if you are also making withdrawals.

• Your IRA may be withdrawn either as one lump sum or in periodic distributions over either your own life expectancy or the combined life expectancy of you and your spouse (if your spouse is your designated beneficiary). Recent rulings provide that you may recalculate your life expectancy annually, so that you won't outlive the IRA proceeds. (You don't have to do the arithmetic; the IRS supplies distribution tables.)

• IRA money is taxable as ordinary income in the year it is received, an important consideration as you weigh lump sum or periodic distribution. It is also counted, in a regulatory turnaround, as part of your taxable estate.

Housing

You may be perfectly content, as you approach retirement, to stay exactly where you are, in a community where you have roots and memories. If so, you won't be the maverick you may think you are. The vast majority of retirees, contrary to popular myth, do not move. Among those who do, most moves are within the same state. Relatively few pick up stakes and move, to the Sunbelt or any other distant locale.

But perhaps you are among those longing after a distant rainbow. If so, now is the time to evaluate a proposed move in terms of both emotional considerations and hard financial facts. Now is also the time to listen closely to your spouse and make a decision based on what you both really want.

Cost considerations may be uppermost in your mind. "We can't afford to maintain this big old house on a retirement income," says an about-to-retire man; "it eats heating oil, the roof will need replacing in a year or two, and then we'll have to paint." "Yes," his wife counters, "but the mortgage is paid up, we'll get a senior citizen discount on property taxes, and we won't be able to buy a smaller place without taking on a high-interest mortgage. Those new variable rate mortgages scare me, especially on a retirement income; we could start out at a lower rate and then, if interest rates go up, be faced with monthly payments we can't afford. That's all we need— to lose a house after we retire!"

As you evaluate costs, consider:

• Your mortgage may be paid up, but it isn't "free" to live in your current house, especially if that house has appreciated significantly in value. What's at stake here is what economists call the "opportunity cost" of money. If your house could be sold today for $200,000 (not at all unlikely, in many parts of the country, if you bought it thirty years ago for $25,000), you have $200,000 tied up in that house. Invested at 10 percent, that $200,000 would bring you $20,000 a year—and that $20,000 a year is what it's costing you to live in that house. Now, of course, you have to live somewhere. But suppose you took the $200,000 you could get for this house and bought a condominium apartment for $120,000; you could buy it free and clear (forgoing most capital gains tax on the profit in your house because you're over age 55 and entitled to the once-in-a-lifetime $125,000 exclusion) and still have $8,000 a year in additional income (the 10 percent interest on the $80,000 you haven't reinvested in housing). Does that sound attractive?

• There are ways of turning your house into a money-making investment while continuing to live in it. Equity conversion is the name of this particular game, as you turn your built-up equity into cash. There are several ways to do so; not all are available everywhere, and some are government programs designed to aid the low-income elderly. Among those which you may want to explore, carefully weighing the risks as well as the advantages, are reverse annuity mortgages, sale/leaseback arrangements, and deferred payment loans. All are complicated and it's vitally important to obtain full disclosure of all the facts and figures, including fees and charges, the schedule of payments, any prepayment or revocation penalties, and so on. You'll want to understand the tax implications and to be as certain as possible of the financial stability of the lender. You'll also want to air the whole idea with your heirs: How will they feel about not inheriting the family homestead? How will you feel about it passing into the hands of strangers? Is there any risk of your outliving the payments and losing the home during your lifetime? If all the answers are satisfactory, if the family is in agreement, and if equity conversion is available where you live, it may be the perfect answer. (More information about specific programs is available in *Turning Home Equity Into Income For Older Americans*, available for $1.25 from the Consumer Information Center, Dept. 130P, Pueblo, CO 81009.)

Emotional considerations may be as important as financial ones, since few objects have as many emotional connotations as the family home. "I don't care what it costs to live here. The kids grew up here; they come back and show their children where they slept and played. There's no way to replace this house." Yet home, to many people, is where you are; people are more important than surroundings. "The 'kids' (they're in their thirties now—I still call them kids) will survive our moving, as long as there is a place for them to sleep when they come to visit." If you've always thought you'd like to move, go ahead and give it a try. Before you do, however, be sure to determine your priorities (no off-the-cuff decisions here) and communicate with the people in your life (unless, of course, you have no close ties as you move into the retirement years). Bear in mind that your children, as well as your spouse, may be distressed if you pull up roots and move far away. But bear in mind, too,

that as long as the children get a fair hearing, you and
your spouse can decide what's best for you.

In determining your priorities, consider the goals you've
set for your retirement years and where they can best
be fulfilled. If you want to take courses and frequent
museums, it should be obvious that a self-contained adult
community located in the southwestern desert may not
fill the bill. If good friends are important to you, think
carefully about leaving old friends behind and starting
anew in a new community. If family is the most important
thing, think twice before moving cross-country to be near
your children; they may move themselves and, even if
they stay put, will be busy with their own lives. Try to
think through all the dimensions of the to-move-or-not-
to-move question before you make a decision. Then, if
you're still not sure, make your move on a trial basis.
Rent a place to live, while you test the waters in a new
community; rent out your old place, meanwhile, to provide some income while keeping it available for your
possible return. Hedging your bets this way may be one
of the smartest moves of all.

Whatever you do, if you're married, you and your
spouse must candidly share your feelings about a move.
Try not to let emotional undercurrents muddy the waters.
Ed, for example, very much wanted to move to a retirement community in Arizona. Knowing how much he
wanted the move, Alison didn't say anything. "How can
I be selfish if it means so much to him? But," she confided
to a friend, "the thought of being buried out there, in a
village of old folks, is driving me nuts." Guilty about
"spoiling" Ed's retirement, Alison didn't speak up. But
it was her retirement, too, and she should have made
her wishes known—before postmove distress almost drove
them apart. A retirement community is more than a place
to live. It's a way of life, and that way of life must satisfy
both husband and wife.

Talk it over before you make a decision. And don't
consider it an either-or matter. There are always alternatives to be arrived at in rational discussion. Ed might

have agreed to spending the winter months in Arizona, for instance, with the balance of the year spent in the Pennsylvania community where they had spent their working years and where their children still resided. Talk *your* wishes through, in terms of your retirement goals, and you should be able to reach consensus.

Estate Planning

If you haven't made a will and organized your estate as you approach the retirement years, now is the time to do so. If you die without doing so, just as if you die without sharing essential financial information, you will sow the seeds of lingering resentment.

If you don't write a will, you will have no say in the distribution of your assets. If you don't write a will, the state will step in and distribute those assets in accordance with state law. That may mean that your surviving spouse will get it all, but it may very well mean something quite different. If you don't write a will, moreover, you will have no say in the person who actually makes the distribution; unless you name an executor the state will appoint an administrator and the fee will come out of your estate. In short, if you don't make a will, you are probably costing your heirs both time and money; with no will an estate takes longer to settle and court fees are generally higher. Is this what you want to do to your family?

If you *do* have a will, be sure it's in line with your current life circumstances and reflects your current wishes. If you've remarried, for example, or moved to a different state, be sure to review your will. If you have adopted children or stepchildren, or if your own children have adopted children or stepchildren, be scrupulous in spelling out your intent in your will. Otherwise you might unwittingly disinherit, for instance, a child you've loved as your own but never legally made your own. Once you think through exactly what you want to do, a competent attorney can help make it happen.

Now that you agree that a carefully drawn will is essential, now that you have vowed to keep your will up to date, there's a further question: Will you discuss the will's content with your children? (Your spouse, of course, knows all about it and has made his or her own will.) Wealthy people, as a matter of course, tell their children what financial provisions have been made. The rest of us often shy away from frank financial discussions. Indeed, says New York attorney Abe Siegel, "Money has replaced sex as the topic that parents are least likely to discuss frankly with their children." But do you really want their inheritance, and the provisions you've made for its distribution, to be a total surprise to your children? Assuming that they are mature enough to handle money, and that you are on reasonably good terms, you will be helping them plan intelligently for their own future well-being by giving them a clue as to your intentions. You may not want to disclose actual amounts—"I hate the thought that they might think me worth more dead than alive, that they'll be hovering at the end"—but you might want to let them know if you've set up any trusts or in any way put strings on when they will receive the property.

Beyond disclosure to your offspring, there is the question of your son(s)- or daughter(s)-in-law. Siegel, writing in *You May Be Losing Your Inheritance*, describes a scenario in which you approve of your children's matrimonial choices, get on well with these in-laws, and love them as if they were your very own . . . yet leave your money to your own children and, when they die, to their children, totally bypassing the son- or daughter-in-law. Think about it. When might this dearly beloved child-in-law need money more than when raising your grandchildren as a single parent? Should being deprived of your estate be added to the grief of untimely widowhood? Is that what you really want? If you are concerned that the child-in-law would remarry and pass your property on to a new spouse, that *is* a risk. But most people in such situations make premarital agreements to protect the children of their first marriages. You might even discuss this possibility in your frank and open discussion.

Be prepared for another layer of complexity if your children are in differing financial circumstances. You may not want to be "unfair" by dividing your assets in unequal shares. Yet being scrupulously fair may not be fair at all. "My older daughter is a successful lawyer, married to a successful businessman; they don't need help. My younger daughter is a teacher, married to an artist; they can use every penny they can get. I love them both," this parent says. "What do I do?" The best solution, if there is an adequate estate, is to arrange matters so that everyone gets something—even the wealthiest of children is hurt by being left out of a parent's will entirely—but the needy child gets more. Then, tactfully, explain what you're doing and why.

If much money is at stake and if all your children are doing well for themselves, you may consider doing one of two things: leaving your money in trust for your grandchildren with the income to your children during their lifetimes; or skipping your children altogether and leaving the money to your grandchildren. Don't do this without first discussing it with your children. And don't be surprised if they think it's a bad idea. As Siegel puts it, "Even though they are doing well financially now, there may be many uncertainties lying in wait for them: inflation, for one thing, or unexpected losses or shifts in the economy, or medical emergencies, or whatever. In a wildly fluctuating world, it would be a mistake to put the family funds permanently out of the reach of those who may, at some point, dearly need them. The grandchildren will be well cared for, and they will, after all, inherit from their own parents."

Trusts are sometimes used, as noted, to bypass children and ensure the distribution of funds to grandchildren. Trusts are also sometimes used to permit the uneven distribution of assets to children; a "sprinkling trust" authorizes the trustee to distribute assets in accordance with individual needs, as for a child who wants to go to graduate school or who has heavy medical expenses. Trusts are also used by some parents to control children beyond the grave. One such couple came to financial planner Sylvia DeWitt convinced that their 36-year-old daughter was irresponsible and her husband a ne'er-do-well. Convinced that the younger couple would never change, they had set up a trust under which no one would ever get the money itself, just the interest. "This couple was so obsessed with their daughter," DeWitt says, "that they ignored their son, a stable responsible family man. I finally convinced them to change the arrangement so that the son will get his share of the money over five years; the daughter—they wouldn't change their minds about her—will get only income and never the principal." This daughter may indeed be irresponsible, but are her parents helping her to become more responsible by denying her an inheritance? What are they saving the money for?

Trusts may also be used to monitor the distribution of assets to a surviving spouse. A newly popular form permits a spouse (usually a husband) to leave assets locked up in an irrevocable trust, with income going to his wife during her lifetime and the principal then going to their children. This kind of trust can make sense in the case of a remarriage, where the intent is to protect the children of the first marriage. But if this is not your situation, I urge you *not* to forbid your spouse any and all control over her financial well-being in the years she may spend without you. Such a trust puts an adult in the position of a child, relying on a trust officer to meet material needs. Such a trust is actually "inhumane," according to Atlanta attorney Harriet H. Harris, and there are other ways to save on taxes (usually the primary stated reason why such trusts are established). "A non-working widow," Harris writes in *Financial Planning*, "has lost not only the most important person in her life, she has lost her source of steady income and the fringe benefits, such as health insurance, that came with it. Her overwhelming concern is to maintain her standard of living—not how much she leaves her children, and certainly not the taxes on her estate." You don't even know what those taxes will be—look how rapidly tax law is changing—so why tie your survivor's hands in the interest of saving taxes?

Tax-saving may only be the expressed reason for establishing a trust. Harris sees other possibilities: the sexism that assumes that women can't manage money, and an overwhelming male ego that does not want "his" money (whose money is it anyway?) to fall into the hands of another man if his widow remarries. If your marriage is a good one, and if you've managed to communicate well about the other issues facing you as you near retirement, you should be able to address this issue openly as well. You should make the effort.

Lifetime planning, using trusts, is another matter. You might establish a living trust, under which you name a trustee to manage your assets in accordance with your instructions, to accomplish any of several aims: to bypass probate, have your affairs managed while you enjoy a trip around the world, or have your affairs managed should you become incapacitated. If you don't want to relinquish any control, by turning assets over to the trust while you're hale and hearty, you can establish a standby trust. The legal forms are signed, but no assets are transferred to the trust. Instead you execute a durable power of attorney under which your assets will be transferred to the trust if and when incapacity occurs.

An ordinary power of attorney, giving someone you delegate the authority to act in your behalf, becomes void the moment you become incapacitated. A durable power of attorney is a special form, containing specific wording so that it remains valid during incompetency or incapacity. Again, if you are reluctant to give up control of your affairs while you're perfectly capable of making your own decisions, you can protect yourself. Place the executed power of attorney in escrow with your attorney, to be used only if the need arises. It is also possible in many states, but not in all, to create a power of attorney which becomes effective only after incapacity; this is called a "springing" power of attorney because it springs to life when it is needed. If you execute this kind of document, whether or not you tie it in with a trust, be sure to specify exactly what will trigger action: certification of incompetency, for example, by two qualified physicians.

In these later years, in anticipation of possible incapacity, it's doubly important to have each spouse in control of separate assets. Give each other power of attorney over those separate assets, and you'll each be able to act for the other. Once you've written your will and worked out a plan for lifetime management, you can put these details behind you and get on with the business of living.

The Children's Hour

There was a time, not so long ago, when we could count on our children for financial and emotional support as we aged. For many people, this is no longer the case. It isn't that our children don't love us but that we have fewer children (in some cases none at all) and that our children have problems of their own. The biggest of these problems may be divorce. The contemporary trend toward serial marriages has created shifting generational configurations that are as yet unexplored. But concern is growing. As Barbara J. Nelson of Princeton University put it in a letter to *The New York Times*, "The children of the 'divorce boom' are just now beginning to grapple with the problems associated with aging, perhaps ailing, parents, stepparents, grandparents and step-grandparents. Where will their loyalties lie? Which of the 'parents' will they want to help, or feel obligated to help? Will they have sufficient financial and emotional resources to go around?"

When the "younger" generation gets divorced, men and women (particularly women) in their twenties, thirties, and even forties, they are likely to turn to parents for help. "I didn't expect to be raising children again at this stage of my life," says a 62-year-old grandmother. "But how can I refuse my daughter this chance to get

started again?" This grandmother wasn't ready to turn
to her daughter for help. But many people in their sixties
and seventies do need some financial help; many more
seek emotional support. Neither may be available to them.
Elderly parents generally cannot count on as much financial support from adult children who are going through
divorce, widowhood or remarriage, a Purdue University
study for the American Association of Retired Persons
found, and those adult children tend to underestimate
other needs of their elderly parents as well. The problem,
not surprisingly, is that men and women experiencing
any of these marital disruptions are often faced with
diminished financial resources of their own; they also are
emotionally drained by the stress in their own lives,
including conflicting responsibilities between job and
home. These adult children may be temporarily blinded
by the pressures in their own lives and not even see the
extent of their parents' emotional or financial need. If
you have several children, of course, it's possible to turn
to others who are not undergoing stress of their own. In
a smaller family, you may not have that luxury.

And what about the situation, not uncommon these
days, when it's a couple in their fifties or sixties who is
getting a divorce? If you turn to your children for support
during this crisis, will they be there again for you later
on? Michael Smyer of the Gerontology Center at The
Pennsylvania State University raises the question: What's
the long-range effect on that young adult child? Twenty
to thirty years down the road will that person, that child,
be willing to put out that kind of effort again when Mom
reaches old age? Or will the child, drained by the earlier
effort, be more distant? "We just don't know," Smyer
says. "But it is clear that the divorce has a ripple effect
up and down the family tree and we're not sure of the
long-term effects."

There are other "ripple effects" if you are the one
contemplating remarriage. Some adult children are able
to welcome your interest in making a new life after divorce
or widowhood. Others are not. They may have not yet

worked through their own feelings about their other parent. They may want your attentions for themselves, as a built-in babysitter for example, and be willing to resort to emotional blackmail to get that attention; children can stir up guilt feelings in parents just as readily as the other way around. Or they may be fearful that your estate, especially if it's sizable, will go to someone else; every potential spouse may be accused by such offspring of being a fortune hunter. Sometimes, unfortunately, the children are right. Often their fears are groundless. If you're convinced that you're doing the right thing, try to talk through the situation with your children. Involve outside help—a clergyman or your attorney—if necessary. But don't let the children dissuade you from a decision that you know is sound. It's your life, your money, and, in the end, your decision to make.

By and large, however, given good family relationships, most children are there when aging parents need them. They are supportive of the idea of remarriage. And they pitch in to provide physical, financial and emotional help as required. Fully 20 percent of the home office employees surveyed by The Travelers Insurance Company (in an attempt to measure care-giving by adult children) are providing some form of care for an older person, typically a mother in her late seventies. Most of the care-givers, in line with expectations, are female. And the help itself varies: More than half the respondents provide companionship, transportation, or help with household chores. Four in ten manage the elderly person's finances, and three in ten provide direct financial support. There's what Smyer calls a "pattern of reciprocity" in which parents and children support each other, as needed, throughout the lifespan. With today's long life spans, in fact, grandchildren are frequently old enough to lend a helping hand.

The Third Generation

What is your relationship with your grandchildren? The "typical" grandparent, the sit-by-the-fire-and-tell-

stories-about-the-past grandparent, hardly exists any more;
he or she has gone the way of the rocking-chair retiree.
Both grandparents and retirees—they're not necessarily
one and the same—are more likely, these days, to be
holding down jobs, doing active volunteer work, or traveling. If you're busy leading your own life, you don't
have time to be an unpaid babysitter. But you do, unless
you're completely atypical, want contact with your
grandchildren. Will that contact consist of gift-giving?
Or will you try to play a role in their lives?

In order to make the most of the grandparent-grand-
child relationship, try to visit with your grandchildren,
at least occasionally, in a one-on-one way. If you live
nearby, encourage the grandchildren to drop in; if you
live at a distance, ask your children to send the grandchildren for a solo visit. But don't feel, however frequently or infrequently you see your grandchildren, that
you must play St. Nicholas. A little grandparental indul-
gence is just fine, but you can't buy their friendship and
you shouldn't want to. If your grandchildren run to greet
you when you visit, collect their presents, and run off,
you may want to rethink the presents. You may be over-
doing it. It may not be immediately apparent but children, even when they appreciate gifts, are far more
appreciative of your interest, and of time spent together.
When you do give gifts, try to make them gifts, personally chosen, instead of money. If you must give money,
give it directly. "My grandmother wants me to have
something 'from her,' she says," a 16-year-old complains,
"but she gives my mother the money and tells her to
pick it out. That's a cop-out."

When grandparents send cash, sadly, it may be because
they don't really know the grandchildren well enough to
know what they would really like. When grandchildren
live several states away, or on another coast, visits may
be few and far between. Sadder still, for many grandparents, is the loss of grandchildren through their parents' death or divorce. Some daughters- and sons-in-law
stay in touch with a first spouse's parents, but many
(especially in the event of divorce) do not. So many

grandparents have been shattered by the loss of their grandchildren in this manner that almost all the states now have laws permitting grandparents to sue for visitation rights. Suing, of course, is a last resort; it's unpleasant, it alienates the middle generation still further, and it costs money. It's better, if at all possible, to reach an amicable agreement. And it's best to reach such an agreement before the divorce even takes place; your own child could include grandparental visitation rights in the divorce settlement.

In later life, both financial needs and emotional needs take on a special character. But planning ahead and talking things over are the keys to successful personal relationships.

Money Traps in the Later Years

• Retirement, no matter how much you may anticipate it, is a major life change and therefore potentially a stressful event. Failure to prepare for retirement in emotional as well as financial terms will make it more stressful.

• If you're married as you approach the retirement years and both of you are employed, your retirement time frame may well be different and will demand resolution. If only one is employed and is now going to retire, you must bear in mind that the at-home spouse has not been living in a vacuum, waiting for you to retire and fill the days. Whatever your circumstances, you owe it to yourselves to consider each other's retirement needs, to share information and to make decisions together.

• Consider your heirs' needs and wishes, as well as your own, as you plan the distribution of your estate. Money, remember, is only one aspect of your legacy— warmth, love, and respect are the rest.

Conclusion

"I MUST have told you about the purple cauliflower," my friend said, as we were discussing what I was writing about in this book. "I don't think so," I replied, "but what's a cauliflower, purple or not, got to do with men, women, and money?"

My friend was in a market one day with her companion, and she admired a magnificent purple cauliflower. In fact, she wanted to buy it. But she had left her own money at home and her loyal companion, the man who had frequently offered to buy her anything she wanted, said, "Three dollars for a cauliflower? That's ridiculous." "I went back a couple of days later and bought it with my own three dollars," she concluded, "but that purple cauliflower is a symbol. I know I have to have money of my own."

It isn't money itself that's important, very often, but the way in which money and the things it buys (whether Tiffany necklaces or purple cauliflowers) interfere with, subtly alter, and sum up our relationships. There's a balance of power in every relationship, no matter how loving, that can easily be tipped by the presence or absence of money. Just as parents can and often do use money to control children, so lovers and spouses can and often do use money to control their partners. Sometimes it's done consciously, sometimes not. But money—the way we use it, discuss it, and react to it throughout our lives— has a profound impact on our personal relationships.

Few relationships, even today, are fully equal. Some are more equal than others, but even in these the balance shifts from time to time. The partner temporarily or permanently in control may exert that control directly,

as in refusing to share either information or cash. Or the
control may be manipulative, as in claiming a purchase
is silly and thereby implying that the would-be purchaser
is equally foolish or in twisting guilt-strings and playing
one-upmanship.

Money arguments, similarly, may be trifling, revolving
around little habits of profligacy or penury that can drive
a partner crazy. Witness the married couple bickering
over scraping unused ketchup back into the bottle or,
conversely, taking too much ketchup and wastefully
throwing it out. Money arguments can be serious,
reflecting deeper problems, as in dissension over credit
abuse or chronic overspending.

Money conflicts, trivial or serious, frequently arise out
of a failure to communicate. Misguided assumptions and
misplaced expectations do more to disrupt relationships
than almost anything else. Don't assume that you know
how your spouse or your lover, your child, or your parent, feels about money. Don't assume that you know
how that person will behave in a given situation. Talk
about it. Discuss where you're going and how you plan
to get there, negotiating compromise where necessary,
and you'll go a long way toward forestalling conflicts over
money.

Money, it's all too clear, is far more than a medium
of exchange. Money is a symbol, representing love and
security and power. Money is a tool, which can be used
in a variety of ways. You can use money in constructive
ways, to enhance a relationship. Or you can use it in
destructive ways, to undermine your relationship and
diminish you both as individuals. Which do you do?
Which do you want?

Take a good hard look at the role of money in your
life and in your intimate relationships. Then move ahead,
together, to make money work for you.

Index

Financial plannner, 212
Financial Planning (Harris),
222
Fishman, Barbara, 117, 127,
128
Fiske, Marjorie, 188
Franck, Linda Bird, 87, 116,
118
*Fresh Starts: Men & Women
After Divorce* (Cauhape),
101
Freud, Sigmund, 60
Friendship, 24–25
Future of Marriage, The
(Bernard), 5

Gagnon, John, 83
Gender, attitudes toward
money and, 5, 39–40
see also Sex roles relating to
money
Generation's influence on
money attitudes, 7–11
Geriatric consultants, 200
Glamour magazine, 7, 11
Goal setting, 67, 82
Goldberg, Lee, 106
Golish, Edy, 107
Good Housekeeping, 26, 173
Goodman, Ellen, 110
Government securities, 69
Grandparents, 123–24, 131,
158, 226–27
leaving money in trust for
grandchildren, 222
visitation rights, 228
Growing Up Divorced
(Francke), 87, 116
Guardian, naming a, 166, 167

Halpern, Dr. Howard, 19, 20,
190
Harris, Harriet H., 222, 223
Health insurance, 71, 108
Heatherington, Mavis, 107

His, Mine and Our (Seifert),
64, 77
Hopkins, Robert, 13
Household expenses:
grown children contributing
to, 193
of live-togethers, 37–40, 43
of married couples, 55, 61–
63, 64, 92–93
Housekeepers, 97, 106, 148,
151
Housing:
costs of, 9–10, 16
divorce settlement and
family home, 87, 90, 94,
98, 105, 130
equity conversion, 216
helping children with down
payments, 188
for live-togethers, 45–48
moving back in with
parents, 106, 191–95
moving out of parents'
home, 17
in retirement years,
214–19
vacation homes, 78, 95
willing a home in a
remarriage, 130, 132
see also Property

Idaho, 73
Identity confusion, 144
Independence, 5, 9, 40, 64,
114, 136, 171, 172
of aging parents, 195–96,
198, 199
parental relationships and,
16–22, 189–95
rate of divorce and
women's, 84
see also Dependency
Individual Retirement
Account (IRA), 97, 214–
15

Institute of Research,
University of Michigan,
22
Insurance, 71–72
disability, 72, 165
health, 71, 108
life, *see* Life Insurance
property, 72
Insurance agents, 212
Internal Revenue Service, 93,
163
Investment Company
Institute, 8, 10
Investments:
in divorce settlements, 94,
95–96
of married couples, 68–69,
78
of singles, 14–15, 31–32
Irrevocable trust, 132, 222–23

Job loss, 185–86
Job training, 86
Job transfers and relocations,
179–80
Johns Hopkins University, 186
Joint and survivor annuity,
213
Joint custody, 99
Joint ownership, 74–77, 90,
130
forms of, 47, 76–77
pros and cons of, 74–78
Joint tenancy, 47, 77

"Kitty" for live-togethers, 38
Klagsbrun, Frances, 128, 173,
183
Kling, Arnold, 9

Langer Report on *The New
Mature Mother*, 135,
144, 156

Later years, *see* Retirement
years
"Law and Marriage: Your
Legal Guide," 161
Lawyers, 201, 212
consulting, 51, 126, 196,
225–26
Leases, names on, 28, 46
Legal matters:
live-togethers and, 35–36,
37, 45–48
obligations of parents, 160–
61
property laws, 72–78
see also Estate planning;
Wills
Levinson, Daniel, 21
Levy, Frank, 9
Life annuity, 213
Life insurance, 48–49, 71, 93,
115, 126, 130, 142, 164–
65, 181, 211
Lifestyles, 16, 87
*Lifetime Book of Money
Management, The*
(Weinstein), 80
Living together, 33–52, 55
bank accounts, 37, 43
charge accounts, 43
contracts, 47–49, 50–51
decisions on mingling your
money, 37–44
housing decisions, 45–47
insurance, 48
money traps in, 52
practical matters, 43–49
property, 44–45, 46, 47,
49–51
sample situations, 34–35
setting the rules before, 35–
37
splitting up, 49–50
stage of life and, 41
as temporary state, 33
wills, 44, 47, 49

Living trust, 223
Loans:
  as business arrangement, 26
  between friends, 25
  mortgage, 46, 212, 216
  record keeping for, 212
  see also Credit
Loss, sudden financial, 185–86
Love, money linked to, 3–4
Louisiana, 73
Lump sum payments of pension benefits, 214

McCall's, 191
Maintenance payments, 83, 91, 96, 109, 130
Making It As a Stepparent (Berman), 116
Marriage and Divorce: A Contemporary Perspective (Bjorksten and Stewart), 59
Marriage and money, 53–82
  budgeting, 68–69, 179
  communicating your expectations, 54, 59, 82
  conflicts over money, 54
  credit, 70–71, 82
  the family financial officer, 66, 82
  insurance, 72
  mid-life matters, *see* Mid-life matters
  money traps to avoid, 81–82
  negotiating, 78–82
  new rules of, 58–60
  parental ties, 60, 189, 194–95
  parenthood, *see* Children; Parenthood
  pooling funds or separate accounts, 62–66
  property amassed during marriage, 72–78
  retirement years, *see* Retirement years
  savings and investments, 68–69, 78
  setting goals and objectives, 67
  sex roles and, 6, 8–11, 36, 40, 54, 57, 58–59, 206, 210, 223
  styles of marriage, 61–62
  wedding bills, 30–31
  see also Divorce; Remarriage
Marriage Contract, The (Weitzman), 119
Married People: Staying Together in the Age of Divorce (Klagsbrun), 128, 173
Marvin, Lee, 49–50
Marvin, Michelle, 50
Maternity leave, 135, 140–41, 146–49
Mediation, divorce, 92
Medical University of Southern California, 59
Medicare and Medicaid, 196
Mendel, Ellen, 196
Mental health, job losses and, 185–86
Men, Women & Change (Scanzoni and Scanzoni), 137
Michaelis, David, 25
Michel, Richard C., 9
Mid-life matters, 142, 169–202
  aging parents, 192–202
  job transfers and relocations, 179–80
  money traps, 201–02
  relations with your children, 187–95, 202
  stay-at-home wives, 180–83

Seifert, Ann, 64, 77
Self-esteem, 25
  of the elderly, 198
  of husbands who earn less
    than their wives, 177–79
  job loss and, 186
  money linked to, 3, 4, 6,
    59, 135–36, 144, 172,
    175
Self magazine, 15
Self-sufficiency, financial, 32
Selsberg, William, 125
Separate accounts, *see* Bank
  accounts; Charge
  accounts; Checking
  accounts
"Separate Property System,"
  65, 77
Series EE bonds, 182
Sex roles relating to money,
  5–7
  dating and, 30
  generation of upbringing
    and, 8–13
  live-togethers and, 35, 36
  in marriage, 5–7, 8–13, 35,
    40, 55, 56, 57–58
  in retirement years, 204–
    06, 210–11, 223
Shaevitz, Marjorie Hansen,
  172
Shaevitz, Dr. Morton H., 172,
  177
Shared-time jobs, 156
Sharing financial information,
  67, 182–83, 210–12, 228
Sheehy, Gail, 174
Shelley, Florence R., 199
Siegel, Abe, 220, 221
Singer, Dr. Laura, 113
Single parents, 97–107, 135
Singles and money, 12–32
  dating, 28–30, 107
  friendships and, 22–26
  money traps, 31–32

parental ties, 16–22, 32,
  191–92
roommate relationships, 26–
  28
single parents, 97–108, 135
stages of, 14–16
wedding bills, 30–31
see also Divorce; Living
  together; Widows and
  widowers
Sloate, Laura, 64
Smith, C. W., 102, 107
Smyer, Michael, 225, 226
Social Security
  Administration, 104
Social Security benefits, 15,
  42
Social Security taxes, 9
Spanier, Graham, B., 42
"Sprinkling" trust, 221
*Stages: The Crises That Shape
  Your Marriage* (Singer),
  113
Standby trust, 223
Stepfamily Association of
  America, 116
Stepparents, *See* Remarriage
Stewart, Thomas J., 59, 79
Stockbrokers, 212
Superwoman Syndrome, The
  (Shaevitz), 172

Tavris, Carol, 81
Taxes, 126, 150, 162
  capital gains, 94, 95, 216
  child care credit, 97, 151–
    52
  estate, 75, 166, 189, 222–23
  rules affecting divorce, 94–
    97
  writing for tax returns, 93
Teenagers in a "blended"
  family, 120–25
Temperament and money, 4–
  5, 54–55, 69